Praise for

"I just loved this book. Told fr[illegible]
has lived sport on all levels—participant, Olympic Champion, coach and parent—Duff's views and perspectives are invaluable and ring true on so many levels. Weaving in personal stories and experiences with lessons learned from teammates, friends and those around him (famous or not), the message and the teachings about values, priorities and defining success in sport are critically important, particularly today. I'm grateful for a book such as this, and truly hope it gets in to the hands of as many athletes, coaches and parents as possible!"

—Beckie Scott, O.C., OLY
2 x Olympic medallist
Former Chair, WADA Athlete Committee
Former member IOC Athletes' Commission

"Niitsi Siáákia'tsisnin. A very unique, and inspiring book. So many great stories, lessons, and advice to inspire many others who live and promote physical literacy in their communities. I'm happy to call Duff Gibson my friend, and someone I admire and respect."

—Rilee ManyBears
Iinomaahka (RunningBuffalo)
2 x World Indigenous Games medallist, cross-country running

"Duff brings his unique insights, experiences, and passion into every chapter of this book. His writing is relatable and engaging and this is the book I wish I could have read ten years ago although I still found myself furiously nodding and note taking at the hidden nuggets throughout."

—Erica Wiebe, OLY
Olympic Champion, freestyle wrestling

"When I started Classroom Champions, it was because I wanted to have an impact and because I believe in the Olympic ideals. That came from my experiences as an athlete. Duff and I were both immersed in sport at a time and place that I think we'll look back on as being very special. There was and is tremendous value in what we lived and learned. *The Tao of Sport* encapsulates that time and a value system that elevates everyone involved. It's as much about character and personal growth as it is about high achievement and I loved reading every page."

—Steve Mesler, OLY
Olympic gold medallist, bobsleigh
Founder, Classroom Champions
Board of Directors,
United States Olympic & Paralympic Committee

"Duff Gibson looks at sport from many different perspectives. That's what makes *The Tao of Sport* such a great and educational read whether you are an athlete, a coach, a parent, all (or none) of the above. I've enjoyed this book very much."

—Dan Jansen, OLY
Olympic gold medallist, speed skating
NBC Analyst, U.S. Olympic Hall of Fame

"Above all else, Duff Gibson is practical about what matters in youth sport, elite sport, and life. As a perceptive student of people, performance, and development, Duff provides rich examples of what makes a difference. He is an amazing observer of life, and draws on experience from a wide range of sports and credible sources. The lessons he shares can be invaluable to young athletes, elite athletes, parents, coaches, and performers in any field. *Loving what you do* and *gratitude* are among the many attributes that can pay rich personal and team dividends. Enjoy!"

—Cal Botterill, PhD
Professor, author, performance psychologist
for various professional and Olympic teams

"*The Tao of Sport* is truly a pleasure to read. Straightforward, honest, and so relatable, Duff shares the stories of his life and the stories of others that have impacted the way he sees the world. Invoking laughter, tears, and deep gratitude throughout, Duff does a wonderful job painting a picture of the value and power of sport."

—Carol Huynh, OLY
2 x Olympic medallist, coach
freestyle wrestling

"The soul of this book is wisdom. Duff Gibson's, *The Tao of Sport* is a fascinating compilation of stories, interviews, and life-lessons that any athlete, coach or parent would find engaging, interesting and useful. I liken reading this book to sitting down with a world class athlete and coach, and hearing their meaningful reflection on what their time on the world stage has meant and taught them. A great read!"

—Jason Dorland, OLY
Coach, author of *Chariots and Horses*
Partner, *Your Mindset Coaching and Consulting*

"As someone who has worked in elite performance sport in Europe and North America for over three decades, I have seen first-hand the behaviours and characteristics of high performers. A key observation is an unwavering mindset that these individuals display through both the incredible heights of success and the inevitable periods of failure and self-criticism that have to be endured. The psychological platform and 'sense of self' are critically important and likely the cornerstone for effective and repeatable performance under any conditions. It is interesting that these aspects of sport/human performance are largely misunderstood and, or, misrepresented, and often neglected despite some excellent resources (knowledgeable individuals and various 'tools'). *The Tao of Sport* takes the reader on a journey of exploration of self through a depth of narrative and storytelling from Duff's own experiences and an array of ideas, examples, and observations provided by an impressive list of his connections. Presented in a highly digestible informal format, Duff's writing provides a wonderfully insightful and important read that contributes greatly to this largely undervalued topic area. Enjoy!"

—Stephen R. Norris, PhD
Former Director of Sport Physiology and Strategic Planning, CSI-Calgary
Performance conversationalist to various corporate, sport, and military groups

"This is the book I wish every sport parent, coach and athlete would read. Duff's deep well of experience and critical reflection makes his perspective remarkable and insightful. His voice and character are inimitable."

—Cari Din, PhD, OLY
Olympic silver medallist, artistic swimming
Teacher and scholar in leadership and coaching
2021 University of Calgary Student Union:
Teaching Excellence Hall of Fame Inductee

"So much of this book instantly reminded me of my own experiences as an athlete, I often felt I was reading my own story. This highlights the power of the many insights Duff shares—that they are universal to achieving success in sport and yet still resonate far beyond. Indeed, anyone reading this book will come away with a deeper understanding of how to pursue excellence in any field. With humility, candour and great detail, Duff peels back the layers of high performance sport to reveal the many factors necessary for success, and in doing so changes our perception of what success really means. *The Tao of Sport* is as entertaining as it is thought-provoking—a must-read for athletes and anyone else interested in achieving great things."

—Kristina Groves, OLY
4 x Olympic medallist, speed skating
Renewable energy consultant

"The athlete in me knows that the message in this book is so true. The coach in me understands how important this message is for young athletes. The parent in me realizes that this book applies to life in general, not just sport. This book is a *must read*."

—Lascelles Brown, OLY
Multiple world and Olympic medallist, bobsleigh
Youth sport coach, professional photographer

"How do you write *the* book on sports? Well for starters, you need phrases of precision and concision. I kept thinking, that this line or that one, would make a great book title. Duff's work is full of more great titles than he won."

—Ron MacLean
Olympic broadcaster
Host, Hockey Night in Canada
Rogers Hometown Hockey

"Duff Gibson has seen sport through so many lenses. His insight into what truly defines a champion is a testament to his experience and passion for what sport gives us. Sport is part of our journey and this journey should be fun. Regardless of what successes and struggles are in our path, sport inspires us, and Duff has witnessed that."

—Catriona Le May Doan, O.C., OLY
2 x Olympic gold medallist
President and CEO, Sport Calgary

THE TAO OF SPORT

REFLECTING on PURPOSE, PASSION, and GROWTH from a HOTBED of HIGH PERFORMANCE

DUFF GIBSON

The Tao of Sport

Book ISBN 978-1-7776414-0-5
Hardcover ISBN 978-1-7776414-4-3
e-book ISBN 978-1-7776414-1-2
Audio ISBN 978-1-7776414-2-9
Other ISBN 978-1-7776414-3-6

(Published by: Duff Gibson in 2021)

For mom and dad who sent us outside and had us figure it out ourselves. For all the leaders, teammates, and competitors. And for Jen, my greatest supporter and the reason I couldn't wait to be home.

So much of what I talk about in this book occurred in and around Moh'kinsstis, and the Treaty 7 territory of southern Alberta. Respectfully, I acknowledge that these are the traditional territories of the Blackfoot Confederacy: the Siksika, Kainai, and Piikani, as well as the Tsuut'ina Nation, the Stoney Nakoda Nation, and the Métis Nation: Region 3. It is my hope that both individually and collectively we move forward, by not only acknowledging, but also by acting deliberately in a manner befitting of reconciliation.

Table of Contents

Introduction

In January of 2002, I was with the national skeleton team in Königssee, Germany, preparing for a World Cup race about a month ahead of the Salt Lake City Olympics. It would be the first time since 1948 that skeleton was again on the Olympic program and the whole sport was going through a transition period. In simple terms, the stakes had been raised. The last few races were of added importance for our men's side in particular. Only the top three nations in the world standings would qualify three athletes each, and we were on the verge of doing so. There was also pressure individually to stay in the top ten to get the best possible ice conditions for the Olympic race itself.

A few days into our training, a psychologist by the name of Matt Brown showed up at the track to continue his work with a few members of our team. We hadn't met at that point but I knew him as a former decathlete, having seen him around the weight room and running track at the Olympic Oval back in Calgary. Because he had the time, Matt was kind enough to offer his services to the other members of our team. Once on site, he made his way to the change room where we awaited the start of the second training run of the day. Matt sat down beside me and asked if he could do anything to help. We still laugh at what were literally the first words I ever spoke to him: "Yes. Don't sit down beside me between training runs at a World Cup and ask me if you can help."

Admittedly, it wasn't my finest moment. But part of the issue was the fact that my teammates and I were dealing with pressure we hadn't felt before. We weren't entirely acting like a team and

I've come to appreciate that everybody pays a price under such circumstances. But I can't entirely blame my response on the environment. I had a terrible attitude about sport psychology! I thought it was something intended to address deficiency, as opposed to a way of building strength. In other words, I fell into a very common trap. I didn't want to show weakness, so I pushed it aside.

My first interaction with Matt revealed my bias, but where did it come from? Why was this one aspect of sport somehow different from any other? It never occurred to me to reject weight training because it was for people who weren't strong enough. Eleven years prior I had graduated with a master's degree in kinesiology from the University of Calgary, which meant I had taken and passed a graduate level course in the subject area. From what I remember, we learned about breathing exercises to control muscular tension, and we learned about negative-thought-stopping. From this brief experience I was rejecting an entire field of study because I saw it as being for people who couldn't handle pressure. It's hard to believe I had risen to the level of representing my country and still hadn't figured this out.

To establish a chronology, my time in high performance sport began as a grad student working under renowned sport-scientist Dr. David Smith. In addition to learning from his expertise, the program was valuable in that it gave me hands-on experience with a number of national teams based in Calgary. From there I transitioned into my own athletic career in which I was able to compete at two Olympics: Salt Lake City in 2002 and then Torino, Italy, in 2006. After the Torino race had gone about as well as I had dreamed it could, and because at age thirty-nine I was old by the standard of elite sport, I retired on the spot and have never once been on a skeleton since.

From there I went straight into coaching, initially at the development level and then in my second year with the national "B" team before taking over as head coach for the four-year Olympic cycle beginning after the Vancouver Olympics in 2010. The most time-consuming aspect of my job related to the technical component of skeleton—how to get down a track in the shortest possible time. That never changed. What *did* change was spending more and more time helping athletes reach their best state of preparedness, in particular for the big races. When it became my job to foster the competitive mindset of others, I had an epiphany about what I had been so quick to dismiss as an athlete. I came to realize that sport psychology, and in a broader sense the mental side of sport, was perhaps the single most important aspect. In my view, this is certainly the case at an Olympic or World Championship level where athletes are under a microscope and races are won and lost by very small margins.

I also came to realize that in my own career, I wasn't successful because I never felt doubt or questioned my own ability—of course I did. In fact, I worried about it all the more because of how athletes are so often portrayed, or how we present ourselves to each other as being *unwaveringly* confident or even *fearless.* I never knew an athlete who was, at least not all the time. What I did have working in my favour was a great deal of time training with, and in proximity to, numerous dedicated and successful athletes. Calgary is truly one of the world's hotbeds of Olympic sport. Success breeds success and I was immersed for the better part of three decades.

I was also helped tremendously by a mindset established when I was much younger, specifically during a time in my youth when I developed a great passion for sport and competition. My parents were the opposite of what is now sometimes referred to as "helicopter" parents, but at the same time they had strong beliefs about raising children. In our house and honestly, throughout the neighbourhood, there was a common belief that if the sun was shining, kids should be outside. We probably would have stayed on the couch and watched TV if we had been allowed to, but as my mom would say, it wasn't "a request".

Once outside, we played street hockey for hours and were very often in trouble for not getting home before the streetlights came on. My personal experience lies almost exclusively with Olympic sport, but having read my share of professional athlete biographies, a common thread seems to be a period of time when their parents had to drag them in off the street at night because they didn't want to stop *playing.*

By the time I was in high school, I wasn't necessarily the top athlete, but I had developed a love of sport and competition, and specifically, for the *challenge* of sport. Perhaps most significantly in terms of a mindset, I was raised to believe it was *just* sport. As Winnipeg journalist Scott Taylor put it, "The great thing about sport is that it enables us to care passionately about something that really doesn't matter." In the big picture I knew sport was of little consequence, so whether I won or lost, it was never going to be a life-changing ordeal. It can't be overstated how much of a *competitive* advantage it is to keep sport in perspective, particularly in those moments when your opponents are feeling the pressure as well. Because I had this awareness, I was never afraid to go up against someone better than me. I almost looked forward to it, and I believed in myself and my ability to be at my best when it mattered most.

If there is an overarching theme to the book it's this: it begins and ends with the *love of the game.* Whether your goal is to enjoy a healthier lifestyle or to be a champion on an international stage, both are predicated on the same foundation. It needs to be something you want to do. It needs to be fun. The first chapter in this book is about youth sport because it's a critical time in terms of establishing this foundation and figuring out what it is that you love to do.

Something else I keep coming back to is the fact that there appears to be commonality in terms of a mindset or a philosophy amongst very successful people. As a master's student and as an athlete and coach, I've had the wonderful opportunity to meet, train with, and learn from athletes who are not only world-class, but in a number of cases world-*leading*. Their athletic accomplishments as well as what many of them have created beyond the realm of sport are a reflection of a mindset. *WickFest, Fast and Female, Spirit North,* and *Classroom Champions* are all incredible programs created by Olympians in just my part of the world. What do the founders of these programs have in common, in addition to Olympic gold? Among other things, it's a sense of gratitude and an awareness of the world beyond themselves—attributes that contributed to their athletic success.

The bottom line is that certain mental characteristics are just too common amongst elite performers for it *not* to be related. This is why I chose *Tao* for the title, a Chinese word which roughly translates to *path* or *way of being*. We have many different paths, but there seems to be a common *way of being*. At the same time, I acknowledge that what I describe in this book isn't necessarily the best *way* for everyone. I can think of one Olympic champion who thought of his competition as the enemy, and later as a coach he encouraged his athletes to do the same. It's what worked for him, but I believe he's the exception that proves the rule. Negative emotions like fear and anger are powerful motivators, but much less sustainable. Sport is not a life and death matter. There are heartbreaking moments to be sure, but overall it's a joyful thing. It comes from passion.

In one sense, this book is just a collection of stories, experiences, and ideas that I've found truth in. That's it. And as a personal philosophy, I would never second-guess someone else's experience or presume to tell them what's right or wrong for them. I'm a big proponent of self-awareness and therefore the goal is for the reader to determine their own truth. I believe there's something to learn from almost everyone we come in contact with, but I would never take someone else's advice over what I knew to be true for myself.

With that in mind, I hope this book inspires thought about mindset and personal growth. I believe emphatically there is a *Tao* that lends itself to personal success as measured both by *extrinsic* factors, like a medal or a championship, and by *intrinsic* factors, like a sense of satisfaction or wellbeing.

If nothing else, if you too share a passion for sport, I hope this book is something you'll enjoy.

1. Strong Foundations

"Of the ten coaches I had as a youth, one made me a better player, three didn't do me any harm, and if I'd listened to the other six, I never would have become a professional football player."

—Marco van Basten

This book is mostly centred around high performance sport, but I talk about youth sport a few times because it's really a foundational time for an athlete. I believe that fostering a growth mindset and *a love of the game* need to be top of mind for youth sport coaches as there are both short- and long-term implications relating to motivation as well as athletic potential.

In my experience, and I've had this conversation with a handful of Olympic-level coaches, it's very difficult to change the mindset of someone in their 20s or 30s. It's something established much earlier than that. Kids start out playing for the fun of it, and if they're lucky, it remains something they love to do, despite the increase in workload as they get older and enter the higher levels. A successful competitive mindset is actually well-aligned with the motivation of a young person *before* they're flooded with such strong messaging about the importance of winning, whether that messaging is intentional or not.

When my youngest son was ten, there were parents on his hockey team who thought of me as the "non-competitive" guy. Sometimes if they didn't realize I was around they said things like, "I hope we win tonight! Oh, sorry." Without being too specific, I'd describe myself as the *opposite* of the non-competitive guy. What the parents were referring to was my expressed belief that we make winning too important in youth sport. Because this argument is often mischaracterized, I need to be clear that I *don't* believe kids should get a trophy for showing up. This practice has been shown to backfire in terms of boosting self-esteem, which is presumably why it exists in the first place. I *am* advocating that we help young people maintain perspective with regard to winning and losing—not to protect them from failure, just to avoid teaching them that it's catastrophic. It's important because it's tied directly to what motivates a young athlete to play and *keep* playing.

About five or six years ago now, my wife and I were at our son's baseball game when I came to realize how a focus on winning can also impede development. I think it just clicked for me because the same play happened twice in one game. As per the rules of Little League, which is for kids aged twelve and under, there are no lead offs until the pitch crosses the plate. Because the kids are young and of a wide range of ability, they're taught to take the lead off every time. If there's a hit, you just keep running towards the next base, and if the ball gets past the catcher, which happens quite regularly *because it's Little League,* you're in a good position to steal a base.

Most often the catcher gets the ball and just throws it back to the pitcher. This of course happens again and again. Runners take a lead off and then casually walk back to the base. If they're too casual about it, sometimes a catcher with a strong arm can throw down to first before the runner gets back to get an *out.* On this day, both teams had their best player behind the plate, and at different times they each tried to pick off a runner at first. I can't recall if the throws were off or if the first baseman wasn't paying attention, but in each case the ball ended up in right field. And again, because it's Little League, the right fielder wasn't paying attention either and the runner was on third base before the ball got back to the infield. The reaction from each coach and each parent was exactly the same. I heard it four times: "Focus on the batter."

In other words, *don't do that.* Don't attempt a play inherent in the sport of baseball. What justification would a Little League coach have for discouraging it? The only possible answer is that winning is the *most* important thing. It makes it harder to win if we allow the base runner to go from first to third. This was a *kid's, regular season, house league,* baseball game. And to my recollection, every team made the playoffs anyway! Kids develop so fast at that age. Wouldn't you want them pushing their limits, at least in the regular season? It makes me wonder how many times a Russell Martin or a Yadi Molina threw a ball into the outfield trying to perfect the move growing up. They would have done so countless times at the major league level as well, but that's beside the point.

This is a very subtle example, but to a kid there's a consistent message here. Winning is important. A lot of people don't see a problem with that. It's a competitive world and we want our kids to be successful. The whole point of competition is to determine a winner. But there *is* a problem, and in a nutshell it's this: you can't make winning really good, without also making losing really bad. The two concepts are tied together. The definition of one is the *absence* of the other. And when you ask kids why they quit—and they quit in large numbers beginning at around age eleven—the number one reason is that it's not fun anymore. It's too serious. It's too much about winning. More obvious examples like bullying a referee who's probably also a kid, or belittling the players when they make mistakes, sends a very clear message that it's *not about fun.*

It's not my intention here to be critical of certain parents or coaches. I understand the passion and I get caught up in it myself. I truly do. I also know that parent volunteers are overwhelmingly great, and with our two sons, sport has been an absolute gift, largely because of the parents they've been lucky enough to have as coaches. But I present this information from the perspective that parents want the best for their kids. And more to the point, if these behaviours arise from a desire to have our kids succeed and potentially achieve a higher level, then the energy is misdirected.

If you take the fun out of sport, kids don't want to play. This part of the argument is cut and dry. There's too much data out there to dispute it. If kids don't want to play, then talent and potential are irrelevant. But again, I'm *not* saying youth sport shouldn't be competitive. I've spent a lot of time convincing my own kids that the fun part *is* the competition. It's also very rewarding to challenge yourself and then see the improvement. The greatest athletes I've known all thrived in a challenging environment. They were *also* the kids who never had the fun taken out of it, and I know this because they still love what they do.

An easy way of keeping it fun is to make it seasonal. By switching from sport to sport over the course of a year, in essence, you leave them wanting more. Early specialization, or playing only one sport for the entire year, has become quite prevalent in the last few decades, and in a sense that's to be expected. Many kids will happily play their favourite sport all year long if we let them. Many parents are afraid their kids will get left behind if they don't. We want the best for them, but early specialization has a number of significant consequences relating to burnout as well as an increased *rate* and *severity* of injury. Something I wouldn't have anticipated is that the earlier you specialize, the more likely you are to lead a sedentary lifestyle after you quit!

Despite these risks, some have argued that sports like hockey and soccer are so technically demanding that in order to compete at an elite level, there's no other option. Based solely on the numbers, this does appear to be true with regard to gymnastics and figure skating, but these are also sports in which there have been world champions at age sixteen and younger, and therefore everything happens earlier, whether that's good or bad. You could also argue that gymnasts *are* multi-sport athletes. With respect to hockey however, the data suggests National Hockey League players typically didn't up the intensity or frequency of training until they were about fourteen, right around when they tended to specialize.

There are undoubtedly successful athletes from almost every sport who were early specializers. However, they are the exception rather than the rule. In a survey of American summer and winter sport athletes who competed in at least one Olympics between 2000 and 2012, athletes averaged three sports per year until age fourteen and 2.2 sports per year until the age of eighteen. Even after eighteen, American Olympic team members still averaged more than one sport per year. Of course if you exclude the gymnasts and figure skaters, those numbers are even higher.

Perhaps the most definitive study ever of high performance sport was published in the European Journal of Sports Science in 2014. Not only was the sample size massive at 1558 athletes, but the calibre was also excellent, involving German national team members from every Olympic sport. The study found the factors contributing to adolescent success were either of no relevance or were *negatively* correlated with success as a senior athlete. In other words, what makes someone a great twelve-year-old athlete either doesn't matter or actually makes them less likely to be successful beyond that point. Specifically, the study concluded that starting earlier, specializing earlier, as well as high-intensity sport-specific training were all shown to be correlated with adolescent success. This might be the single biggest reason why it persists. Playing one sport for the entire year, whether we push them to do it or they're begging us to play, *really works.* Unfortunately the benefits are fleeting.

In contrast, world-class senior athletes typically started later, specialized later, and played many other sports prior to specializing. Essentially, it's the opposite set of conditions. The study also found no relationship between hours of practice in their primary sport as an adolescent and how successful they were as a senior athlete. These results were found to be consistent over time and independent of sport. In addition to burnout and the increased risk of injury with early specialization, according to this study, it's actually counterproductive to senior level success.

So with all the negative, why are we even having the conversation? The biggest driver remains the short term benefits for young athletes, and therefore it's not hard to find coaches and teams in support of the concept. Then you have the profit-driven industries that have arisen to cater to the demand. This is not to say that youth sport programs are inherently bad—absolutely not. But there are, in fact, very few people promoting early specialization who don't also benefit from the belief that it's a good thing…or perhaps a child's only hope. At the very least, when it comes to *your* kids, it would be worth the time to seek out advice from someone not associated with a youth sport program or team.

The one aspect that seems to fly under the radar is athleticism. If you've played a variety of sports, you're a better athlete. You've built a foundation that lends itself to *all* sports. I've personally heard the manager of a AAA baseball team, which is one step below the major leagues, say they're not looking for ball players—they're looking for athletes. They believed they could teach the baseball part, but there's only so much you can do if there's a deficit of speed, strength, balance, or coordination. This is also why you have a storied hockey coach like Brent Sutter saying he can tell the difference between multi-sport athletes and those who have only played hockey. Multi-sport athletes have, in essence, better prepared themselves for novel environments. I once saw a clip of Steven Stamkos, captain of the Tampa Bay Lightning, lurking at the side of the net as a shot was taken. The rebound went straight up in the air, Stamkos choked up on his stick and scored through a very narrow gap, with a motion similar to a bunt in baseball. The point is that the move is not something you would ever practice in a hockey environment. Young athletes succeed largely because of early skill acquisition. As athletes get older and the technical proficiency starts to even out, it becomes very difficult to hide a lack of athleticism.

In summary, specializing in one sport before at least fourteen is not an effective strategy to help kids one day achieve their true athletic potential. In fact, it might be stacking the odds against it. As we better understand the research and its implications, it's my hope that parents will begin to make changes in the best interest of their children from *within* organizations. My friend and former teammate, Nathan Cicoria, is in the process of doing this with his daughter's soccer club. Instead of the organization constantly fighting with families who want their kids to play other sports in addition to soccer, he has proposed they transition into Calgary's first soccer *and* hockey club. He's getting some support and I really hope it happens because it's a brilliant idea and I think a number of organizations may follow suit.

Sometimes we forget the original purpose of sport and why we have our kids involved. It's of value to re-examine such things from time to time. Without question, there are competing forces involved. But if the goal is for our kids to love what they do and lead healthier active lives, and in the process learn those life-lessons about dedication and teamwork, then multi-sport is the foundation. If the goal is for our kids to be the best they can be, then it's no different.

* * *

"Whoever said winning isn't everything probably didn't win."

When I first saw this anonymous quote on a social media platform, it had been shared over two thousand times. This kind of thing is popular because it typifies an attitude people connect with very quickly. It generates an *instinctive* reaction that by its nature requires little time or thought. This is how we experience sport. A goal is scored and there's an immediate sense of elation or disappointment. There's no analysis or interpretation in the moment. It's a *reaction.* But let's be clear about it—that quote is bravado. Given the purpose of professional sport however, you could argue it's not inappropriate within those bounds. At the same time, it's completely inappropriate with regard to youth sport given *its* purpose and specifically what motivates a young athlete.

You might think this quote, or others like "second is the first loser", is harmless; they're only words after all. But when they begin to creep into a mindset, they become counterproductive for all levels of sport, for a few reasons including the emphasis on the negative. It is an accepted truth in the realm of sport psychology that trying to have a good performance is vastly more effective than trying *not* to have a poor one. Being your best requires a focus on what you are trying to achieve, not on the outcome you're hoping to avoid. To consider second place a *failure* isn't a realistic standard. In the course of an athletic career, twentieth is sometimes an unqualified triumph. The mindset is also counterproductive in the sense that it changes the focus to outcome when the path to a successful outcome is an effective *process.* A coach doesn't call a timeout in the heat of a playoff game to tell the team to win; they talk about strategy and execution, which is process.

After the Sochi Olympics I stepped away from coaching so I could spend more time with my kids and be a bigger part of their sporting experiences. In so doing, I came face to face with a great deal of intensity and negativity directed at very young athletes. It wasn't necessarily *our* coaches or parents, but it was present at the rink and at the field almost every time. Presumably, parents and coaches push their kids because they want them to be successful, but ironically, and I say this as the former head coach of an Olympic team, *we* would never have tolerated it! If we had had a coach or parent behaving this way, we literally would have had them removed from the program. We would have seen it for what it was—disruptive and of no value. Yet it seems to be acceptable with regard to our kids. I have a vivid memory of my youngest son commenting after a game that his coach took it "way too seriously". What is it about this environment that leaves an adult oblivious to what is perfectly obvious to an eight-year-old?

Youth sport should be about two things: learning and fun. And here's something that would surprise a lot of people: sport at the highest level is *exactly* the same. Think of it like this: if you want to be the best on the planet, it's all about getting a little better each day. To do so, you need to be a student of your sport. Hard work is a necessary but not a sufficient condition of success. In other words, you can't just show up and blindly go through the motions. You need to think and study and learn. A great training program is very methodical with regard to exercise physiology, skill development, strategy, diet, recuperation, *all of it,* and a great athlete needs to understand and participate fully.

It also needs to be fun. Admittedly what a youth and a senior-level athlete considers fun are two different things, and it's important to appreciate this fact. But the bottom line is that, in both cases, there needs to be something that makes them *want to come back*. The greatest athletes I've known have all been very passionate about their sport and they love to challenge themselves. They weren't the kids who were taught that losing is something to be ashamed of. They were the ones who had an innate love of what they did. That doesn't happen by accident and it has nothing to do with wins and losses. "Second is the first loser" flies in the face of a philosophy that not only makes kids more likely to participate, but more likely to be successful. As I mentioned before, if kids don't want to play, then talent and potential are irrelevant.

I think back to when I was a kid and it was almost the best possible scenario. Admittedly, we didn't have an Xbox or a cell phone to distract us, but sport was a big part of our lives. We played road hockey for hours at a time after school and on the weekends. Sessions began with the careful selection of teams, followed by the obligatory argument about who got to be the Leafs. Ironically, the "winners" of the argument got to be the Leafs while the "losers" had to settle for the Islanders, a team in the midst of winning four consecutive Stanley Cups. We then had subsequent arguments as to who got to be our favourite players, but of course pretending to be Darryl Sittler or Mike Bossy was part of the fun. We didn't have uniforms, and we didn't have grown-ups telling us what we were doing right or wrong. We were left to figure it out ourselves, and we loved it for its own sake.

The recommended standard in North America for kids aged five through seventeen is sixty minutes of moderate to vigorous physical activity per day. Regardless of the jurisdiction, a dishearteningly small fraction of kids are meeting this standard. In my neighbourhood, it would have been difficult to *stop*. I can recall on more than one occasion someone going to get a new fluorescent tennis ball so we could see it better in the dark and keep playing. This was despite our parents' instructions to be home by the time the street lights came on. It was great fun, and all these years later, I still see it the same way.

During those road hockey games, I believe it was of particular significance that we didn't keep score. In fact, we gave no thought to the score at all until enough people had to leave that it meant the end of the game, at which point came the familiar, "Next goal wins!" It was the perfect combination of fun and excitement without any concern, let alone *fear* of failure. We likely wouldn't have expressed it this way, but we thrived on the challenge. We competed against each other with great intensity because *that* was the fun part.

There was actually one situation in which we did keep score. When we had too many kids to have a single game, or if we only had one net, we would make three teams and have shorter games to three or five goals with the winning team staying in and the losing team switching out. Even though we kept score in this scenario, it was still notably different from organized sport in the sense that if one team beat another by a large margin, we would rearrange the teams. We wanted it to be as even as possible because that raised the level of competition. If it was only about winning, wouldn't we have had the better team arguing not to change it up? We never did. We *did* occasionally have an argument initiated by the team on the wrong end of the score *insisting* they didn't need the help.

It was a very healthy way of looking at sport. We came to understand that scoring was great fun and *trying to win* was the point of competition, but there was certainly nothing shameful about getting scored on. *And* there was something you could do about it. You could try again and you could try harder. The better the team you faced, the harder it was to score, and the more likely you were to get scored on. As a consequence, it was a greater achievement when you did score. You had to earn it.

If everyone thought this way, or if we actually *taught* it this way, how many fewer kids would believe they didn't *like* sports, or *competition*? Do they really not like these things or were they taught not to like them? This is a concept that has a direct impact on a young person's desire to participate, which in turn has long-term health implications, let alone on who might stick with it and ultimately reach an elite level. Show me a great athlete and I'll show you someone who was never taught to be humiliated by failure, which is of course something absolutely inherent in sport. I want my kids to see how rewarding (and therefore fun) it can be to face a challenge and perhaps not succeed initially, but keep trying and learning and growing and then maybe succeed the next time. I just don't want the wins and losses interfering with the great value sport can be for them.

So how or why does it happen? Parents don't intentionally take the fun out of sport. There's no one who *wants* that, but it happens because we're passionate about our kids and we want them to be winners. Sometimes we get caught up in the moment. There are others who actually want their kids to *hate* losing as presumably this is a motivation to win. Unfortunately, for so many kids, this is not what happens at all. If we create an environment where kids begin to see losing as humiliating, it doesn't usually make them try harder. Kids often adapt by *avoiding* situations in which they might lose! If we want our kids to be successful, we should want them to seek out tougher competition. We should encourage them to challenge themselves. Of course, if you challenge yourself by facing a better opponent, you're more likely to lose. Placing such an emphasis on winning is actually teaching our kids to avoid the challenge, not seek it out. Carol Dweck's research about *growth* versus *fixed* mindset, which I speak about in more depth in Chapter 4, bears this out.

Because it's such a formative time, what we're teaching a young person about *competition* is something every coach needs to be cognizant of. The wins and losses simply cannot be allowed to interfere with an innate love of the game—something so intimately associated with long-term potential *as well as* fun and participation.

2. Nature and Nurture

"I am somehow less interested in the weight and convolutions of Einstein's brain than I am in the near certainty that people of equal talent have lived and died in cotton fields and sweatshops."

—Stephen Jay Gould

The term "nature/nurture" refers to the fact that every last one of us is a product of both genetics and environment, or in simpler terms, what we were born with and what we do with it. The phrase is sometimes expressed as "nature versus nurture" or "the nature/nurture debate", and while scientists of various genres argue as to the extent, there's no debate at all about the fact that both play a significant role in human development and your potential to excel at a given pursuit.

To be successful at almost anything, you need passion, dedication, and a belief in yourself. With regard to sport in particular, there is also an undeniable genetic component. If the goal is to be great at the 100m sprint or the marathon or at rebounding a basketball, you can't get to any significant level unless you're actually built to do those things—and then believe in yourself and work really, really hard for years and years.

The need for what is commonly referred to as "good genetics" varies according to the demands of a given sport. With certain team sports, of which baseball and hockey are good examples, you have elite performers of all shapes and sizes. The average height in the National Hockey League is about 6'1" but you also have Zdeno Chara at 6'9", a six-time all-star and record holder for the hardest shot. In Major League Baseball you have an average height of about 6'2" and then there's Jose Altuvé. The Houston Astros sign stealing controversy aside, he's an undeniably elite player with both offensive and defensive awards to his credit at 5'6".

In these and other team sports, you see the variability in part because of the high skill component involved. It's not uncommon to have a baseball player who is an obviously poor runner and yet is still a significant asset to a team because they are also an elite pitcher or hitter. Similarly, in hockey there are players who rarely score but are just as valuable without the puck in preventing the opposition from scoring. Within any given team sport, you often have athletes of various sizes and shapes in part because they have a different skill set and they're actually doing different things. There might not appear to be one specific body type, but there are very definitely physical characteristics that lend themselves to aspects within a sport.

It's also true that genetic suitability is often a subtle thing. Sometimes it's completely invisible. For example, research conducted in the Human Performance Lab at the University of Calgary in the late 1980s when I first arrived as a student, found the top sprint speed skaters in the nation on average actually had a shorter thigh bone relative to overall leg length. Presumably a shorter femur means better leverage with respect to the gluteal and upper hamstring muscles. I'm not aware if this relationship was ever examined beyond that one study, but I know a shorter femur is also considered "good genetics" in the world of power lifting. My point is only that the relative length of the thigh bone just isn't something that's visibly obvious.

A better example might relate to pitching in baseball. There are some readily apparent characteristics that lend themselves to throwing speed, such as shoulder and elbow flexibility and arm length in both absolute terms and relative to height. There are also hidden anatomical traits that have to do with internal moment arms and the nature and location of muscular attachments, generally relating to the geometry of the shoulder and elbow. These are internal physical traits that are rarely measured. And why would you? You measure how fast someone can throw a baseball. It's easy to look at Randy Johnson or Aroldis Chapman and see they were built to pitch—they're physically awesome. It's not as obvious when you look at Tim Lincecum, who was listed at 5'11", or Marcus Stroman at 5'7". The truth is they were absolutely built to pitch as well. You just can't see the anatomical traits that make this so.

The best example I have as it relates to pitching might actually be a friend of mine who's never played baseball. Paul Boehm is my former teammate from the national skeleton team. He finished fourth at the Torino Olympics and won more than his share of World Cup medals during his career. Years ago, if memory serves it was the year after Torino and at the same track, when a World Cup race got snowed out. When it was cancelled, all that nervous energy that would have gone into racing erupted into a giant snowball fight. After the fact, it was the consensus that you really did not want to be on the opposing team from Paul. People were scared by how hard he could throw a snowball!

The following summer, Paul happened upon a booth at the Calgary Stampede where you could throw a baseball at a radar gun, and he threw it 85mph! He just walked up cold and gave it a try. What if he practiced? Or *trained*? Or even just warmed up? Paul never played a sport involving throwing, let alone baseball. I'm quite comfortable saying whatever anatomical traits are associated with pitching speed, he has them. And the only way you would know this is if you happened to be in a particular snowball fight.

Something that's also intimately associated with team sports is the strategic aspect. There is certainly strategy involved with individual sports, but the variability of a wide field of play and several teammates working together is just *different*. Steve Nash was certainly quick, but undersized and only average in terms of his athletic ability, speaking specifically in the context of professional basketball (no disrespect intended—actually *respect* intended). Yet he was twice the National Basketball Association's MVP because of his ball handling skills, awareness, and moreover, his ability to control a game and execute a strategy. This is very similar to some of the all-time great hockey players like Wayne Gretzky or Sidney Crosby. Both were considered the best player on the planet at different times and neither was ever thought of as being the biggest, the strongest, the fastest, or having the hardest shot. So because of the strategic aspect of team sports, genetics is still relevant, but less so.

On the other end of the spectrum you have the sports that are only about one thing, like who can go higher, throw farther or cover the distance in a shorter time. With these sports in particular, there are very specific anatomical traits without which you simply cannot compete at an elite level. It's not enough to love something and really want to get to the top. We are all built a certain way that lends itself to particular sports and not to others. All the men and women in the 100m final at the Olympics, for example, are literally incapable of being elite marathon runners because of a variety of genetic characteristics, including a higher percentage of fast twitch muscle fibres. This is not to imply elite sprinters don't train every bit as hard as other athletes, but you are either born to sprint or you are not. The same could be said of elite marathon runners but on the other end of the spectrum. They are physically *incapable* of being elite sprinters.

Some wonderful examples of genetic suitability are the legendary swimmers Ian Thorpe and Michael Phelps. Both had an advantage over almost anyone they competed against because of their proportions. This is not meant to undercut their achievements; it is only to say they were doing what they were born to do. For example, Ian Thorpe has size seventeen feet! If you're like the average adult male with size nine or ten, then you might as well race against someone wearing flippers. Michael Phelps too has huge feet, hyper-mobile ankles and shoulders, and an oddly long torso and wingspan relative to his height. David Epstein goes into significant detail about Phelps in *The Sports Gene* and it's nothing short of fascinating. Before you take into account the incredible amount of quality training with the best coaches, trainers, medical staff, and so on, these guys are already untouchable compared to the average person. It's no different than someone who is of average height trying to win a tip off against someone who is seven feet tall. You can train and *believe* all you want, but it's not going to change the outcome.

I realize this flies in the face of a commonly held belief. There is no shortage of those who would tell you that you can achieve anything you put your mind to. It seems as though winning a championship is the prime opportunity to promote this belief. Kevin Garnett screaming, "Anything is possible!" after winning the 2008 NBA Championship comes to mind. To me, this was the ultimate example of an athlete who had trained and sweated and dedicated his entire life to reach the pinnacle...of a sport he may as well have been genetically engineered to play.

I suppose if you spend your childhood dreaming of hoisting the Larry O'Brien trophy, to then actually do so must seem like you've achieved the impossible. And truly, if literally millions of young people are dreaming this same dream, you've defied the odds. But the reality is that for every situation in which many people are vying for the same goal, be it a championship trophy, Olympic gold, or a Nobel prize, regardless of the odds, someone has to win. It must seem miraculous to win the lottery but they're going to keep drawing numbers until someone does—it's the nature of it. The difference is, in sport, there's a high proportion of competitors who have long since bowed out because of innate physical characteristics.

To be clear, believing in yourself is an absolutely valid and critical component of being successful, in the context of sport and beyond. Perhaps in an effort to achieve a wider appeal, this concept is often presented in an overly superficial manner, almost like the stereotype of what people assume it to be. Why might that be? In psychology there's something referred to as the *fun•amental attribution error.* It means we want to assign a dispositional explanation for behaviour. If someone does something good or bad, we tend to attribute it to unchanging mental characteristics, much more so than the myriad of physical traits or other circumstances beyond their control. There's some really interesting research showing almost every one of us will tell a lie under certain very specific conditions (specific to the individual), if we think we'll get away with it. But if we catch someone in a lie, we put them in a box. They're a *liar.* Someone who commits a crime is a *criminal.* It works the other way as well. Someone who is successful is assumed to be that way because of drive or determination or brilliance—all of which are certainly relevant but not to the exclusion of circumstance.

How this translates to sport seems to vary according to the demands of the event, and sadly there is evidence to suggest it also varies according to the race of the athlete. A lot has been written about how commentators and journalists refer to black versus white quarterbacks for example. But again, in general terms, we tend to default towards a dispositional explanation. During Michael Phelps' comeback at the 2016 Olympics in Rio, commentators repeatedly referred to work ethic, training environment and mental toughness. Each of these is absolutely valid, just not to the exclusion of genetics, which played an equally large (or larger) role.

The bottom line is that it will always be a combination of both nature and nurture. And it's almost always more complicated than in the manner in which it's discussed. It's never as simple as *trying harder* or *believing in yourself*. These clichés are intended to be inspirational. They suggest anything is possible, which is a strong motivator if presented with the right nuance or if you *haven't* tried really hard or you haven't believed in yourself *yet*. But for those who have, the unintended implication is that a lack of success is a result of a deficiency in effort or belief.

I did my undergrad at Western University in London, Ontario, and competed in rowing for the four years I was there. The main competitive season was in the fall but there was a spring season as well, culminating at the storied Dad Vail regatta in Philadelphia. On one of those spring teams, in an effort to inspire us for the final few days of the competition, our coach gave us each a copy of an article written by, of all people, Arnold Schwarzenegger. In it, he said that even at the age of sixteen he knew that he had the potential to become Mr. Olympia, essentially the world champion of professional bodybuilding. Our coach gave this to us as an example of great willpower and positive thought. However, in my case at least, I didn't connect with the message.

Part of the issue was that it was too big of a gap between bodybuilding and what we were doing as a university rowing team. Also, I had seen a picture of Schwarzenegger at sixteen, and he looked slightly less defined perhaps but every bit as big and muscular as he did when he won Mr. Olympia only seven years later. The implication was that *believing* had brought about these miraculous changes, but how hard was it for him to believe when he looked like *that* at sixteen? That was hardly miraculous. Show me the Mr. Olympia who weighed 98 pounds at sixteen! It was like believing you could win the 100m at the Olympics if you were running ten seconds flat in high school. It's not exactly a stretch of the imagination.

Reading about other athletes can be tremendously inspiring but there needs to be some commonality, some way of seeing yourself in the other. I would assume that "try to be more like Arnold Schwarzenegger" misses the mark for most. And yet, *believe in yourself* is such a valid and universal message. I was just never personally motivated by the advice of a celebrity, or the marketing department of a shoe company. *My* passion for what *I do* is the only relevant perspective, regardless of what might have been said this morning by an "influencer" on social media.

The whole concept is a bit of a chicken-or-the-egg scenario. Does *believing* affect your ability to perform? It absolutely does in the sense that it's tied to your confidence, or lack thereof. I'm not sure if it's as simple as Henry Ford's, "Whether you think you can, or you think you can't—you're right." The quote implies that *believing* brings about the reality. At the same time, any social scientist would tell you the best predictor of future behaviour is your own past behaviour. High performers intuitively know this.

My confidence as it applied to an upcoming race was always directly tied to my speed in the training runs leading up to it.

Before the Torino Olympic race, my worst rank in training was fourth, and that was without a race-calibre start. In that sense the Ford quote applies, but it wasn't the believing that led to the performance—it was the past performance (in my case the training runs) that led to the believing *and* the performance. That's part of the reason why there isn't a chapter about *believing* in this book. It's something I touch on here and there but *believing* is an outcome arising from previous experience as much as it is a part of the process moving forward. Though it does beg the question of what you do when the training runs don't go well.

* * *

Determining your suitability for different sports is yet another argument for a multi-sport upbringing. We are all suited for some things and very definitely *not* suited for others. A distinctly different challenge is finding what you love to do. This is a more important question for two reasons. First, the purpose of youth sport is not to fast-track athletes to professional or Olympic sport. It's about values and lessons and promoting an active and healthy lifestyle. That's why it *exists.* It's really about wellness, and therefore fun is more relevant than someone's possibly misguided impression about who has "potential".

Second, whether the goal is to play for fun or ultimately to compete at the highest level, fun is a necessary requirement. Fun, or in other words, what *motivates* a young person, is sometimes overlooked within the higher ranks of youth sport. As a result very talented and ambitious young players decide to quit before any kind of potential can be determined. The numbers alone should be a wake-up call to reprioritize the goals of youth sport organizations, but to this point the cycle seems doomed to repeat.

Perhaps this is to be expected as parents cycle in and out of coaching as their own children get involved and then age out or quit. As the guru Dr. Steve Norris points out, the quandary of the entire sport system is that we have our most precious resource working with our least experienced people.

For a young person, determining what they love to do is typically easier to figure out, and if they're lucky, there's some overlap with what they're genetically suited to. Sometimes kids love to do certain sports in part *because* they're suited to them. The point is simply that they're two separate and distinct questions. It's a wonderful thing for a young person to get out and try a variety of activities (sport or otherwise) to find their passion and gain a sense of their strengths and weaknesses. Keep in mind that when talking about genetic suitability as it relates to sport, any conclusions drawn before puberty are more or less irrelevant.

And to be sure, there are going to be failures along the way, but what a shame it would be to give up the search, never having found one's true calling. From a statistical perspective, there's a kid out there with as much potential as a Christine Sinclair or a Sydney Crosby or a Penny Oleksiak who'll never try soccer or hockey or swimming. I have no doubt there's also a kid somewhere with the untapped ability of a Margaret Atwood or a Celine Dion who never chooses that path or gets the opportunity. Being *great* involves a tremendous amount of hard work, which is why it's about finding your passion. Finding your passion is about getting out there and being open to new experiences.

As I re-read my words here, I'm struck by how harsh this must sound to a young athlete. So in that light, there are a few things to remember. First, if the goal is to be a good high-school-level athlete, then genetics almost doesn't matter. I say *almost,* because there are times and places when high school sport is truly elite—LeBron James as a seventeen-year-old comes to mind. Second, as I alluded to earlier, if you play a team sport, there's a lot of room to be successful even if you don't perfectly fit the mould *or the stereotype* of the mould.

More to the point, there's such great value in sport for all ages and ability levels. The main focus should be to teach sound fundamentals and make it fun in the hopes that young athletes want to keep coming back. Any higher level success would be gravy on top of that. The stat so often thrown around is that 70% of kids quit youth sport by age thirteen. As mentioned above, and despite what many might think, you have very little sense of true athletic potential before puberty. You could put together an impressive list of superstar athletes that never showed any hint of what was to come when they were thirteen *or older*. Michael Jordan would be at the top of the list, but it's a *long* list. I'm certainly not comparing myself to any of these athletes but when I think back to when I was fourteen, I wrestled in the 97 pound category! I weighed about 205 as an adult when I competed internationally in skeleton, so at fourteen I was literally *half* the athlete I would one day become.

It's also important to remember that genetic suitability works both ways. The fact that you are more suited to certain things is also what makes you *less* suited to others. But that should never be used as an excuse not to try a new sport or training method to round out your physical abilities. Shaquille O'Neal is perhaps the greatest all-time "big man" of his sport, but this also makes him horribly unsuited for anything relying on aerobic capacity or a high strength to weight ratio. In other words, Shaq would have been the laughing stock of the steeplechase or the high bar, and I wouldn't hesitate to pick my son at age three over him in a pull up contest. If, however, we look at rebounding a basketball, even now walking out of the broadcast studio several years removed from his playing career, against almost anybody out there, my money is still on him.

* * *

All of this is not to diminish the role of *nurture,* and when speaking in terms of athletic performance, nurture means what you can do *right now* to get better. It means mental and physical *training*. You can't avoid the fact that you need to put in the time. Hard work is a foundational concept for success in sport, or any discipline for that matter, and I can tell you from personal experience that even athletes of a national team calibre vary greatly in their ability to dedicate themselves at a consistently high level. The following is what some former athletes of mine have referred to as my "Dan Gable speech". "Speech" is an exaggeration; it really comes down to a question.

For those who are unfamiliar with the name, Dan Gable is largely considered to be the best amateur wrestler of all time, with absolutely dominant world and Olympic wins in the early 1970s. Despite the fact that as a high school wrestler I wore the Asics "Dan Gable" autographed wrestling boot, there's really no such thing as a celebrity from a rarely televised amateur sport. Within the community however, Dan Gable was and remains the stuff of legend, who took discipline and mental toughness to another level. His motivation to become a champion came shortly after taking up the sport in middle school. In one of his first matches, against an older and stronger opponent, he didn't just lose, he was so physically exhausted he was unable to continue. This was such a humiliating experience for him that he *vowed to never again sleep at night without first exhausting himself from training!*

Now, if this was anybody else, such a declaration would be nothing if not comical. But in this case, it appears to be exactly what he did! From that point forward, Dan Gable went undefeated through high school and then went 117–1 in college, losing only the very last match of his NCAA career to a very talented opponent by the name of Larry Owings. In *A Season on the Mat* by Nolan Zavoral, Gable admits the loss still haunted him long after his career had ended, but at the same time acknowledges its importance in terms of making him re-evaluate his routine and forcing him to work even harder. Leading up to the 1972 Olympics, Gable trained at a high intensity for seven hours *every single day for two years.* Again, you hear an outlandish statement like this and you naturally question the validity of it, but by all accounts this appears to be literally what he did.

The loss to Owings occurred in 1970, but from that point until claiming gold at the 1972 Olympics in Munich, Gable wasn't just *un•efeate•*, he only gave up a few points in total over that entire span. Specifically, in the twenty-one matches in which he qualified for the US team, and then subsequently won the Olympics, Gable outscored his opponents by a score of 130–1. The single point he conceded was during a 7–1 victory over Larry Owings in the final match of the US team trials. It was truly an amazing accomplishment that frankly very few people could ever truly appreciate.

After retiring, Gable had an equally impressive record as a coach at the University of Iowa, and to this day still gets asked by up-and-coming wrestlers what they need to do to become the best. These young athletes are often state or even national age group champions, and yet Gable's answer is the same. "Ask yourself if you really want to be the best." Almost any young athlete would say they would. But when it comes right down to it, in Gable's experience, most aren't willing to do what it takes and/or slowly lose interest as the improvements become harder and harder to come by.

Given the standard Gable set for himself and the hours of training he put in for years at a time, apparently without a break or an easing off in terms of intensity, I can only imagine what it must have been like wrestling for him at the University of Iowa. How would you like to tell *that* guy you've got an injury or you're feeling a little burnt out? What Gable did in his career sounds like folklore, and perhaps over the years it has become an exaggerated version of the truth, but I've always liked sharing the story, if only as a colourful way to make a point.

* * *

So now we've established that if the goal is to be world-class or world-*leading* in sport, it takes a consistent level of dedication that most aren't willing to undertake. Or perhaps some are willing in terms of the physical training but not in terms of recuperation or diet or mental preparation. It needs to be an all-consuming effort or ultimately it's just going through the motions. But for the sake of argument, let's assume the dedication is there. How much work are we talking about?

I think back to a book I was fascinated with called *Outliers* by Malcolm Gladwell. In it, Gladwell refers to extremely successful people from many different fields, from athletes to lawyers to computer programmers to violinists. He talks a lot about the value of hard work and how necessary it is to achieve the absolute highest level. That was the first time I had heard about Anders Ericsson's *10,000 hour rule.* Apparently his research kept pointing to this same number—10,000 hours of specific, targeted practice.

In other words, it takes that much time and effort to reach what is referred to as a "genius" level of a given skill.

In terms of Ericsson's research, what I found most interesting was that in the one study of violinists from a school in Berlin, there appeared to be *no* exceptions. Thirty musicians were divided into three groups of ten according to their ability. Those in the bottom group were likely to become music teachers while those in the middle group were good enough to play in an orchestra. Those in the top group were considered the elite, who might one day solo with some of the world's top orchestras. As it was presented, groups defined by their ability *exactly* matched the total number of hours they had dedicated to the violin over the course of their lives. There appeared to be no exceptions, no "naturals" who relied on sheer talent to be in a group higher than the amount of hours they had put in. Similarly, there were no "grinders", or students who put in the highest level of work to just maintain the bottom or middle tier.

Now, all these years later, it appears as though the data wasn't as cut and dry as it was first presented. David Epstein mentioned in one of his *Range Reports* that there was in fact some overlap between the groups. A few from the middle group had actually outworked a few in the top. Also, in my opinion, the psychology of self-reported numbers needs to be taken into account. If you were a violinist in the top group and it took a few decades of hard work to get there, you'd be proud of your effort. You likely wouldn't *underestimate* the total number of hours. Conversely, you might very well underestimate the number to protect your ego if you were in the bottom group. This is only speculation on my part, but it could have had the effect of artificially separating the groups based on the level of proficiency and *not* by actual hours of training.

Having said that, Ericsson's research still makes a very strong point in support of talent as a product of hard work, or as subsequent authors have said, as being about myelin on nerve cells. But to then conclude natural talent has nothing to do with it? In very practical and *human* terms, natural talent still comes into play, if only through its influence on how you wish to spend your time. Keeping with the violin, if you struggled from the first moment you picked up the instrument and only made a horrible screeching sound, even after a number of lessons, how likely are you to dedicate yourself to it? You'd fit perfectly into the model because you'd never put any significant effort towards something you believed you'd never be great at. Conversely, if you found with only a few lessons you could produce a nice sound and could begin to string notes together, you might find it to be a positive experience. If it made sense to you, if it just felt right, you might really get into it.

Natural talent affects our ability to dedicate ourselves to something. It's not the only factor, but really taking to something and really enjoying it is significant. This is why talent can't be overlooked in terms of achieving the highest level of a particular discipline. Or to put it another way in relation to Ericsson's work, *of course* there are no examples of people who put 10,000 hours into developing a skill who don't reach the highest level. If you had no natural talent for it, why would you torture yourself?

An example that illustrates the point well is the musician Joe Jackson, known for his hit songs *Is She Really Going Out With Him?* and *Stepping Out.* Although being classically trained in composition at London's Royal Academy of Music, and being an accomplished pianist, by his own admission Jackson had tried on several occasions to learn the guitar without success. If it's only about effort, how is that possible? This is a guy who knows about discipline and practice, who understands everything there is to know about musical composition, and who is actually an expert at an instrument where each hand plays a different progression at the same time! Whether it's a keyboard, a chessboard or a football field, some things are just going to feel right and some things are going to be an uphill battle from the start.

Over the years I have found at least four different authors who each referred to Ericsson's work and this specific study from the music school in Berlin. In addition to the previously mentioned Gladwell and Epstein, there was Geoffrey Colvin and Daniel Coyle, both of whom refer to the study in support of the argument that talent is really about specific, targeted practice. This is of course a very positive and motivational message. It's akin to the "anything is possible" narrative which is regularly promoted both in and outside the context of sport. We tell this to our kids when we talk about what they can achieve in their lives. Chris Rock puts a more realistic spin on it with, "You can be anything you're *good* at...as long as they're hiring...and even then it helps to know somebody."

For *anything* to be possible in sport, heart and grit and determination would have to trump genetics, when in reality the absence of either is a deal-breaker (to varying degrees depending on the nature of the sport). Having said that, I don't disagree with what these authors are saying. I just see their message in a slightly different context. In a world where many people would tell you that *nature* is king, these authors are making the case for *nurture.* Truly, there are no elite performers who don't put in the years, while at the same time, there does appear, at least superficially, to be elite performers who are not genetically suited to what they do. As discussed previously, it ties back to the specific demands of the sport and sometimes the genetic aspect is hidden. Skill is absolutely about myelin on nerve cells. It's just not *only* about myelin.

Do I believe in the concept of 10,000 hours of work necessary to achieve the highest level of proficiency for a given skill? In general terms, yes. But apparently the number varies somewhat according to the specific sport or activity. Is hard work a mandatory component to achieving the highest level in sport or any other field? Absolutely. But is it just about specific, targeted hard work and nothing else? No. Again, it's a *necessary* but not a *sufficient* condition. Geoffrey Colvin uses the example of Tom Brady being one of the best in the last two minutes of a football game—a point which is hard to argue with. It seems doubtful however, that the *only* explanation for this is that he works harder than *any* other quarterback in the league, *ever.* If only it were that simple!

A long time ago now, I had a roommate by the name of Richard Young. For many years he competed internationally in track cycling and actually won the sprint event at the 1991 PanAm Games in Havana, Cuba. More recently he was a director with High Performance Sport New Zealand and now he consults internationally. I'll quote him because I haven't heard it put better. He said, "I don't think working really, really hard, day after day and year after year is anything special, because at the highest level that's what everybody does."

He's right. He's absolutely right. At that level, that is what everybody does. But doesn't that contradict the Dan Gable "speech" and the whole idea of outworking the competition? Maybe on the surface it does, but there's a distinction between *getting to* the highest level and outworking people *at* the highest level. Dan Gable was talking to young wrestlers about *getting there.* To distinguish between athletes at the highest level, my own take on it is this: when it comes to what you might call *homework*, as in visualization or studying a specific opponent, you can probably outwork a lot of people, even at the highest level. Admittedly this is where Tom Brady might separate himself from the vast majority of his competitors. If, however, we're talking about anaerobic sports, lactic acid tolerance, *pain* tolerance, then I think you can probably outwork a lot of people, but maybe not so much at the *highest* level.

What many people don't appreciate, relating back to Richard's quote, applies more to energy system sports, in other words, races. At the highest level there, almost everyone is already walking the fine line between working really hard and *overtraining*. This is why diet and therapy and general recuperation between training sessions becomes more and more important. Again, it comes back to the demands of the sport, but sometimes it's not possible to outwork the competition because everyone is already working really, really hard day after day. In fact, some people are working *too* hard and their bodies will react by getting injured or getting sick.

Richard was a world-class cyclist for a reason: working that hard and dedicating years of your life to one singular pursuit is exceptional by almost anybody's standard. But Richard held himself to the highest standard, as elite competitors do. So then if everybody works extremely hard, what is it that separates one from the other? Wouldn't it be great if I could give a definitive answer to this question? Here goes—it takes dedication, hard work, perseverance, belief in yourself, and character. To varying degrees depending on the sport, you also need good genetics. You need nature *and* nurture. You need to be good at the things you can measure, and you need to be good at the things you can't. You also need a good team and a good support system both within and outside the sport. It also really helps to have great passion for what you're trying to accomplish because then you'll daydream about previously unknown ways you can improve.

If you can do all that, then all you have left are circumstances, luck…and intangibles!

Duff Gibson

3. Seeking a Challenge

"[The race] wouldn't be worth a damn if all the best drivers weren't there."

—A. J. Foyt after lending a car to Al Unser at the Indy 500

I remember years ago listening to an interview in which the iconic Olympian Clara Hughes, talked about her cycling career and the satisfaction she felt at the end of a race. She described a situation in which she finished tenth and was absolutely thrilled with the result. She also talked about winning races and being only content because she had met her expectations. For her, it came back to what she had to endure to achieve the result. If she had to work really hard to catch a breakaway group, or if by chance she was slowed by a crash, a top ten result might have been much more significant than a win on another day or in another set of circumstances. For her the harder she had to work for something, the more satisfaction she felt in its achievement. It wasn't only about the rank beside her name.

I've heard this same sentiment expressed many times and in many ways. "The greater the effort, the greater the reward." "If it was easy, everyone would do it." One of my favourites is, "Without challenge, there is no *achievement*." This lesson took many years for me to appreciate. Eventually I realized my success was largely a product of the fact that I love to challenge myself. I'm still very motivated by the process of first setting a goal and then training and working to get better and slowly seeing the progress. I also acknowledge and appreciate those athletes and teams who were better than me for providing the challenge that was a necessary component of my development as both athlete and person.

When I went to my second Olympics, my wife emailed our friends and family and asked them to contribute to a book of messages I could read while I was there. Someone who contributed was a friend of ours named Neal Marshall, a three-time Olympian and two-time world record holder in long track speed skating. He also happened to be Cindy Klassen's coach during her five-medal performance in Torino—in other words, a pretty decent résumé. Neal's message, word for word, was this:

> I just finished reading a book called *Into The Wild* by Jon Krakauer and there was an awesome quote in it that applies to sport and what you are about to do at the Olympics. It reads: "A challenge where a successful outcome is assured is no challenge at all." If you were sure that you were going to do awesome then there would be no fun in it! There would be no reward or satisfaction in it! The whole purpose of sport is to challenge ourselves to accomplish what we know MIGHT be possible. The competition between athletes is really about who can believe the most and create the best chance at what may be.

What I love about Neal's message is that it expresses the fact that our greatest triumphs are when we face the greatest obstacles: the times when, by all accounts, we maybe *shouldn't* succeed. When the odds are against you, the only option you have is to prepare to the best of your ability and go for it. If it was easy, or even remotely comfortable, success wouldn't hold the same meaning or value.

This is admittedly a difficult concept to buy into if you're someone who still has a long road to travel. If you're not ranked near the top, you've got all the challenge you can handle and you might not see it in the same light. For those few at the top, the longer they've been there, the more likely they are to appreciate the struggle itself. As inferred in the Krakauer quote, there are those who are so keenly aware of the value of a great challenge, they choose a path precisely *because* it's more difficult.

In the world of sport, there are a few rare examples of athletes who are so dominant within their own category or event, they actually move to seek out the tougher competition. Certain professional boxers, like Manny Pacquiao, have competed in multiple weight categories after having thoroughly dominated their own. One could argue that in the professional realm, the motivation might be at least partially financial. In amateur sport, with only few exceptions, the motivation has to come from somewhere else.

Many years ago now, I was a volunteer coach for the Calgary Junior Wheelchair Track Club. On one occasion they were able to get Jeff Adams to come to town for a training camp. For those unfamiliar with the name, in the sport of wheelchair track, there was a time when Jeff was really *the* guy. Not only had he won numerous world and Paralympic medals, he was (and remains) a great advocate for the *abilities* of people with disabilities. A number of years ago, Jeff actually climbed Toronto's CN Tower *in a wheelchair.* I feel as though I should pause for a moment so the people reading this for the first time can take it in. Just imagine using only your upper body and core strength to not only pick up your own body weight but also the weight of a wheelchair strapped around your waist. Then repeat that close to two thousand times. To complete the task, Jeff adapted a wheelchair by extending the two front wheels such that the chair sat level on two consecutive stairs. He then put one hand on the inner railing of the stairwell and on the other forearm he held a crutch such that he could push himself up one stair at a time for the many hours it took. I don't want to over-dramatize things (if that were possible here), but I consider such a feat to be pretty close to superhuman.

In any case, in the world of wheelchair track, Jeff was about the biggest name out there (this was early on in Chantal Petitclerc's career). We had athletes down from Edmonton and there were even a few from Saskatchewan and B.C. who came to work with Jeff and learn from his experiences. The most poignant moment of the camp came during a question and answer session when someone asked Jeff about the 1998 World Championships from which he had recently returned. Apparently there was a rule limiting each athlete to three events. The group wanted to know what events he had chosen and why. His answer was simply put. He entered the 200m because he wanted to race Hakan Ericsson of Sweden, who was the fastest sprinter in the world. He entered the 5000m because he wanted to race Heinz Frei of Switzerland, who was the premier long distance wheelchair racer in the world. And he entered the 1500m because it remains the true *main event* in wheelchair track where both the sprinters and distance athletes compete with an equal opportunity to win. Jeff won gold in two out of the three events, but more to the point, he did not choose the events that best suited his abilities. He chose the events that presented the greatest challenge.

The only other example I've ever come across of an elite amateur athlete going to where the competition was harder (as opposed to the rest of us who play to our strengths) is the wrestler Christine Nordhagen. After winning her fourth World

Championship gold in 1998, I can only assume the thought of chasing a fifth title in the same category did not hold the same appeal. Instead she decided to move from 68 to 75 kilograms to challenge a few women in particular who were considered by many to be the best pound-for-pound wrestlers of *any* category. Seven kilograms is a lot of weight, and at least initially Christine was competing against women who were both bigger and stronger. Her first World Championship medal at 75 kilograms was a bronze in 1999, but evidently she was up to the challenge, winning her fifth world title in 2000.

I've come in contact with some truly incredible athletes over the years, but Jeff Adams and Christine Nordhagen stand apart in that they changed categories to seek out greater competition *at a world level.* In these two cases, winning another World Championship gold medal did not present enough of a challenge as compared to actually seeking out the opportunity to be the best of the best.

* * *

It would be exceedingly difficult to reach your full potential without being challenged, and in that sense an athlete is indebted to their competition. This is as true in business as it is in sport.

The book *Good to Great* was a study of publicly traded companies. Because they were public, Jim Collins and his research team had access to numerous articles and interviews, as well as to any and all financial information. Their first step was to define what they considered *great,* and then they went looking for companies that fit the criteria. By their own standard, they were only able to come up with eleven, and the book is in essence a comparison between those companies and ones they deemed as just *good*. The comparison companies were in the same industries, at the same time with roughly the same potential for greatness, but for whatever reason did not take the final step.

Collins talks a lot about Kimberly-Clark (a "great" paper company) and Scott Paper (a "good" paper company) and how they faced the threat of Proctor & Gamble taking over the industry in the late 1960s. Apparently, Scott immediately resigned itself to second place and looked for ways to diversify to try to remain profitable in the face of the challenge. Kimberly-Clark had a completely different approach:

> At one internal gathering, Darwin Smith stood up and started his talk by saying, 'Okay, I want everyone to rise in a moment of silence.' Everyone looked around, wondering what Darwin was up to. Did someone die? And so after a moment of confusion, they all stood up and stared at their shoes in reverent silence. After an appropriate pause, Smith looked out at the group and said in a sombre tone, 'That was a moment of silence for P&G.' The place went bananas. Blair White, a director who witnessed the incident, said, 'He had everyone wound up in this thing, all up and down the company, right down to the plant floor. We were taking on Goliath!'

When I first read the book, I was struck by how it was, as the author suggested, not just a book about business, but also about human characteristics. Clearly, competing against the best brought out the best in Kimberly-Clark. How you see the competition is a reflection of a mindset, and is relevant in any kind of competitive environment, in business or in sport. At the same time, benefitting from great competitors is something you need to be careful with. Goals are most effective when they're challenging but attainable. Certainly for a younger or less-experienced athlete, it's possible to set the bar too high too soon. But the greater risk would be a *lack* of a worthy opponent, or better yet, several. Being a big fish in a little pond, and not realizing it, is not a formula for success and is often accompanied by a rude awakening.

* * *

There's another key aspect to the *effort versus reward* relationship and it ties back to sportsmanship. Especially towards the end of my career, I'd truly had enough of the travel associated with the World Cup circuit. People assume that if you've had a race in Germany, you've actually *seen* Germany. In reality, all you see firsthand is the airport, the highway, the hotel room, and the venue. You usually get one day off per week but that's when you travel to the next race.

There were aspects of the circuit that I could have done without but something I really enjoyed was the people. The friendships I made and the sportsmanship of my competitors played a huge role in my athletic career. In addition to my teammates, there was a core group of five or six athletes from around the world that I had great respect for, due to both their athletic ability and their character. One of those athletes was Gregor Staehli.

Now retired, Gregor was a skeleton slider from Switzerland, and, until very recently, the most successful athlete in the history of our sport. I think it's important to mention his success as it may have played a role in terms of the attitude he had about competition. He won his first World Championship medal in 1990 and won his first World Championship gold in 1994. The year after winning bronze at the Torino Olympics, Gregor won his second World Championship gold medal on his home track in St. Moritz in what I assumed would be his last race. However, after taking the 2007/2008 season off, Gregor returned to the World Cup circuit and claimed his third world title in 2009. In a sport where they have only one big race per year, he has won a total of eight World Championship and two Olympic medals. I won't try to guess how many World Cups he's won, but it's a lot. Probably the single most impressive statistic about Gregor is the fact that if you added up every one of his World Cup races over his entire career, he averaged a fourth place finish! It doesn't get any better than that.

Gregor had been sliding and winning for many years before I met him so I can't say if his attitude developed over time or if it had always been the same. But when you've won so often and for so many years, what value does competition still hold for you? What makes you keep striving to get better? Clearly it has nothing to do with winning yet another medal or trophy. The answer is: the *challenge.* And when you realize the great joy of sport lies in the challenge, you also realize that the better the competitors are, the greater the challenge, and therefore the greater the sense of satisfaction if you are able to succeed.

Another way of expressing it is: if there was no challenge, if it was *easy,* success would be meaningless. How rewarding would it be for a guy with Gregor's résumé to win because his chief rivals had an off day? For him, is that something worth writing home about? No. And to be clear, I've had this conversation with him so I'm not speculating. When Gregor Staehli wished you luck, he truly wanted you to have your best race. Then if you did and he beat you, that *meant* something.

As a consequence, I can tell you firsthand it created this tremendous atmosphere in which to compete *and* achieve your best performance. Competing against Gregor was an honour and pleasure, and on the few occasions that I was able to beat him, he was always very sincere in his congratulations. After my first win at the World Cup level, what made that experience even greater was the support and sincere happiness that some of my competitors had for *my* success, and Gregor was a big part of that.

Ultimately I learned the greatest joy of sport for me also lies in the challenge. When you come to this realization, you can wish your competitors well and even help them perform to the best of their abilities. In the end what you're also doing is adding to your own experience and sense of accomplishment.

Sportsmanship isn't counterintuitive to competition—it welcomes it, encourages it, and perhaps most significantly, it has no *fear* of it. As a consequence, when an athlete adopts this mindset, they compete with a clear focus on aspects of the sport that are within their control, and in the end dramatically improve their likelihood of success.

* * *

The following piece is a contribution from Olympic rower Ben Rutledge. It's about the process of selecting the men's eight that went on to win gold at the 2008 Olympics in Beijing. It talks about the challenging environment and how your attitude towards the other competitors leads to greater performances both individually and as a team.

> The process of finding athletes who can survive in this sort of environment is not an easy task and is the reason we have an

"open camp". Basically, any rower who has at least shown a certain level of skill or potential is allowed to train alongside the best rowers in the country. The top rowers/athletes are given Mike's [Spracklen's] full attention and the best equipment. These rowers then received the opportunity to represent their nation at the World Championships or Olympic Games. Newcomers often think that incumbents are protective or territorial about their positions. In fact, the opposite was true. My teammates and I were always excited if a good new athlete came into the mix that had potential. We saw them as having something to offer the program that could elevate all of our end games.

In 2007 this athlete was Jake Wetzel. He was a 2004 Olympic silver medallist who had taken the previous two years off to sort out an injury and work on his PhD. Jake was a talented athlete who had demonstrated in the past he had the capability to be the best in the world, his team having missed gold by only eight hundredths of a second in Athens.

Our training group at the time was filled with strong and talented athletes, but had not had a top performance in two years. In addition, we had some new young talent in the group that had yet to reach their full potential. This was an opportunity for all of us to come together and start making something gel. In January, Jake arrived, three months after the camp had opened and we were gearing up for our Olympic qualifying year. Competition was fierce to get into the top boats, which would have the best chance at a medal at the World Championships and Olympic qualification.

Jake was a threat to many of the athletes, including myself, since he rowed on the starboard side. In sweep rowing we each only have one oar and it takes time to develop a specific side, similar to hockey or golf. However, we knew if we could harness Jake's power and expertise we would all be better off, even the athletes not selected for the crew. I will try to explain this: We are all now going to try harder to ensure we are not the last guy selected to the crew so if and when Jake gets back up to speed we would not get ousted from the boat—in effect, allowing all of us to push harder than would have been achieved prior to Jake's arrival.

Now I can imagine this might be intuitive in most teams' selections; bring in the good, out with the bad, overall everyone seems better. However, rowing is one of a few unique team events in that it is timed. No goals, no referees, no special teams, no power-play; less random chance is involved, just pure performance. So for those on the team who perhaps saw their opportunity for rowing in the men's eight slipping away with Jake's arrival, they were still given the opportunity to grow in the open camp. They would then try for another boat with the opportunity to prove that if he was good enough to win a gold medal in the eight, he was then also good enough to win a medal in the four or pair. No farm teams, no minor leagues, just a different position on the lake to fine tune your abilities.

By March our eight was doing well, and it had just won the first World Cup of the season. And our boat was an early contender for gold at the World Championships, four months away. Jake had only been training for four months at this point and was not exactly in top form, but our coach recommended the team accept him due to his past performances and athletic talent. Now for some, this meant they were going to be taken out of the boat and possibly their chances of becoming a world champion would be lost. But for others left in the boat this meant they had a chance at reviving a proven performer who could add to the performance of a crew.

In the end, Jake lived up to his past performances and was selected for the team. He was later able to step into a leadership position within the team. That year we won the World Championships by the largest margin in the men's eight event in over twenty years. In relative terms, our margin of victory was comparable to that of sprinter, and fellow gold medallist, Usain Bolt.

Nothing stopped our team from looking at ways to improve, even if it meant putting our own spot on the team at risk. We were dedicated to our team's success and if there was an individual that was going to elevate us, we would explore the possibility. We sat on the start line in Beijing believing we were ready to perform at our best only because the combined beliefs within ourselves, teammates, coach and training program allowed us to do so. This came from a unique program that made us accept responsibility for our own performances and give respect to others.

And with that we claimed the top position at the 2008 Beijing Olympics, even if it meant a few bowels coming loose along the way.

—Ben Rutledge

* * *

Jungle Jim Hunter was one of the original *Crazy Canucks* as a member of the Canadian alpine ski team in the early-to-mid 1970s. More recently, Jim hosted a radio talk show that focused on amateur sport and how to become both a better athlete and person. It was one of the few places where they talked about character and values and how those things actually translated into performance. At one point, Jim invited me on the program to talk about the sport of skeleton and to discuss the upcoming Olympics that were only a few weeks away at the time.

We talked about a variety of topics, one of which was *earning* your results. Jim made the observation that too many young athletes want to "win by default". What he meant was there's a difference between *deserving* to win because you had a great performance on the day and winning because your competitors had a bad day or were unlucky or perhaps had inferior conditions or equipment to work with. There will always be factors beyond your control, but the level of competition contributes to the meaning of a given accomplishment. Very seasoned and successful athletes often appreciate this relationship and want their competitors to be at their best to make it more meaningful should they ultimately prevail. Jim's point was that too many young athletes don't yet appreciate this relationship and would feel happy to win, even in the absence of the top competitors, hence the expression "winning by default".

To illustrate the other end of the spectrum, and what he feels athletes should aspire to, he told a story from when he was a teenager and just beginning his international career as a skier. Because he wanted to be the best, he sought out the best. This led him to meet, train with, and learn from some of the most iconic skiers of all time, including Franz Klammer, Jean-Claude Killy, and Ingemar Stenmark.

What Jim told me next I found to be extraordinary, and while he was telling me, I asked him to clarify more than once. What he did was actually go to the hometowns of these giants of his sport in the off season and literally *show up at their front door unannounced*. He would explain who he was and that he wanted to be a great skier. He asked if he could interview them and try to learn from them what it takes to be great. Apparently he did this on a number of occasions with many of the top skiers of his generation, and incredibly, *he was welcomed in and given valuable information* on almost every occasion.

I have to say, I absolutely *love* this story. I have often wondered why you don't see this kind of thing more often, especially in Calgary where so many national teams are based. I made Jim stick around after the radio program for a good forty-five minutes so he could tell me more about these wonderful unannounced visits. The one that summed up his point the best was the time he knocked on Ingemar Stenmark's door.

As I understand it, the man himself answered, which in itself is beautiful. You can just knock on a door somewhere and the greatest slalom and GS skier of all time with eighty-four World Cup *gold* medals opens the door. If that was the storyline of a Hollywood movie, you'd roll your eyes! But Ingemar Stenmark answered his front door, and after hearing Jim's explanation as to why he was there, asked him if he had his workout clothing with him. Jim indicated he did and was told to come around back for a workout that was just beginning. Jim was able to participate in the session and learned several training techniques that at one point involved riding *unicycles* of various heights uphill through pylons to build both strength and balance at the same time.

At the end of the training, Jim asked Stenmark, "Why did you help me?"

His answer offers great insight into the way a champion of his stature thinks. "I want you to be your best, so that if I win, I can say I was *the* best."

4. Growth Through Failure

"Why waste time proving over and over how great you are, when you could be getting better?"

—Carol Dweck

A discussion about failure, and specifically about *learning* and *growing* from failure, hinges on the research of Carol Dweck. In my experience, most people have a general understanding of her work, or at least the definitions. Someone with a *fixed* mindset believes athletic talent—speaking here in the context of sport—is something you're either born with or you aren't. Someone with a *growth* mindset believes it's something that improves with the work you put into it. The real significance of the concept however, which isn't nearly as well-known or understood, *relates to failure.*

Someone with a *fixed* mindset finds failure humiliating because they believe it exposes a lack of talent, which is seen as an innate and unchangeable quality. With this mindset, losing is something very personal and therefore every athletic contest becomes a proving ground. This aspect of the concept is sometimes challenged by those who believe that *hating failure* is actually a good thing and a characteristic of successful people, which frankly, isn't a baseless idea. We know that negative emotion, and fear in particular, is a very strong motivator. There have been many elite athletes who have talked about the negative emotion of a significant loss staying with them a lot longer than the positive emotion from a significant win.

However, hating failure as a motivator breaks down quickly for young athletes because *not having fun* is the overwhelming reason why they quit sport entirely. I've actually had parents tell me they're happy when their kids cry after a loss because it's a sign they *really want to win.* Every kid is different of course, but being humiliated by something that happens approximately half of the time is a formula for driving kids out of sport, not motivating them. So it's something parents and coaches need to be aware of.

Additionally, what is often missed in this discussion is the fact that someone with a growth mindset might very well *hate failure* as much as someone with a fixed mindset. I feel as though I should repeat that. Someone with a growth mindset might hate failure as much as someone with a fixed mindset; it's just not perceived as something which reveals a personal limitation. It's not *personally* humiliating. Nobody enjoys failure, but the difference between the two mindsets is revealed in what happens next.

Dweck's overall conclusion was that people with a fixed mindset are typically less successful because they tend to avoid situations in which they might lose. In other words, for the fixed mindset, hating failure doesn't result in working really, really hard to try to get better. It actually results in avoiding the challenge. Negative emotion, and fear of failure, is a very powerful motivator, but with this mindset, it turns out the motivation is not to grow but to *avoid*.

This is not the case for those with a growth mindset, and therefore it's important for coaches of young athletes in particular to understand the difference and to know how to cultivate the one over the other. This is actually a very simple process that involves rewarding and reinforcing growth and dispositional characteristics such as work ethic and character over outcome.

Outcome and *who's number one* will always be something a young person is aware of because it's how the world operates. Ask any kid who's the best in their class at school *at anything* and they can tell you. As a society, we celebrate the champion and assume fourth place to be a terrible disappointment. What we fail to realize is that the champion is the one who reacted to failure by trying to get better and by craving another opportunity to challenge themselves.

The child with the fixed mindset was led to believe they were successful because they had "talent". Keep in mind, judging talent and believing a youngster is destined for greatness only because they are better than other U10 or U12 kids is no measure at all. There have certainly been elite senior athletes who were the best at every level along the way, but this is the exception, not the rule. Success in sport before puberty is largely a product of who started first, who grew first, and who did it more often, *none of which correlates with senior level success.*

The athlete who best exemplifies a growth mindset could very well be Michael Jordan. He's a wonderful example, in part because of his oft talked about competitiveness—in a game, in practice, golfing, playing cards, etc. Someone who loves to compete has a very particular view of failure: they don't like it, but they have no fear of it. Moreover, they love the challenge and they thrive in the competitive environment. Think about the fact that Jordan quit basketball after three straight NBA titles and at the absolute peak of his ability to essentially start over in a sport he hadn't played since he was a kid. You don't do that if you're afraid of failure or you're afraid to challenge yourself.

Jordan is also a wonderful example of the growth mindset because, like almost every other great athlete, there was a formative period when he very definitely *wasn't* the best. There's a guy by the name of Clifton Herring who's a basketball coach in Wilmington, North Carolina. Herring, in some circles at least, is famous for being the guy who cut Michael Jordan. I've seen interviews with him rolling his eyes and saying, "Yeah, I'm the guy." Apparently in grade ten, a 5'11" and much-less-skilled Jordan was cut from his high school team. It was just three years later when the 6'6" version became only the fourth freshman in University of North Carolina history to win a starting position for legendary coach Dean Smith and was, in the opinion of those who know more than me, playing at an NBA level. A few years later, Jordan led the 1984 US Olympic team to gold before winning rookie of the year and an all-star selection in his first year with the Chicago Bulls. That's a pretty quick turnaround!

According to Jordan, being cut had a very significant and ongoing impact on his basketball career because it's what first motivated him to work harder. He admitted originally he was trying to prove Coach Herring wrong, but it became much more significant than that. Had he not been cut at that moment in his development, and had he not reacted to the setback in the way he did, would he have become the same player? Perhaps, or perhaps not. Jordan himself certainly gives the experience a lot of credit in terms of his progression.

Getting cut from a team is a significant setback, but sport is something that forces you to face failure and adversity in many different ways and on a consistent basis. Every loss, every injury, every *setback* is valuable because it teaches. This is a mindset that Jordan clearly embraced during his playing career as was expressed in a commercial put out by Nike in 1997. I'd recommend looking it up if you're not familiar. The message is presented very simply and yet powerfully, and it is without question an important message, especially for young athletes when a growth mindset needs to be cultivated.

Visually, the scene is Jordan walking in slow motion into the United Centre in Chicago. The narration is Jordan also. "I've missed more than nine thousand shots in my career. I've lost almost three hundred games. Twenty-six times I've been trusted to take the game winning shot, and missed. I've failed over and over and over again in my life, and that is why I succeed."

People think of Jordan as some kind of machine, this legend who never missed. He was the sport's greatest athlete, who decided he also wanted to win the three-point contest at the all-star game, and did. I think of that commercial and what strikes me is that you can actually string together almost a third of a season worth of games where the NBA Champion Chicago Bulls lost for *no reason* other than the greatest player in the history of the sport missed the last shot. And those numbers were specific to the time the commercial was made. In other words they weren't career totals, and now that he's retired, the numbers are all significantly higher.

I think it's great to look at people who are number one in their field and every once in a while get a little reminder they make mistakes, as we all do. It's valuable to see that all great champions aren't without flaws. But how they view failure and how they react to it is what sets them apart, at least in terms of a mental framework that very clearly lends itself to failing less than the competition.

* * *

"If you want to increase your success rate, you should double your failure rate."

—Thomas Watson, Sr.

"Always make new mistakes."

—Esther Dyson

The focus of sport, both in training and in competition, is very heavy on the negative. We don't tend to think of it in those terms, but sport is won and lost based on the frequency and timing of errors. Did the defence fail to clear the zone? Did the bobsled tap the wall coming out of the corner? Did the figure skater two-foot the landing? In fact, if you ever have the occasion to meet a figure skater who can do a triple axel, ask them how many times they fell before they did it for the first time, or before they were able to do it consistently. The number is typically in the *thousands,* but of course the vast majority would never get to that level. Either way, it's so important to regularly acknowledge *progress* because we spend so much time focused on what went wrong.

In the sliding sports, races are often won and lost by very small fractions of a second. In fact, luge is even measured to the *thousandth* of a second, and on occasion it actually takes that close a look to determine a winner. The second World Cup skeleton race I ever competed in was in Austria where I finished tied to the hundredth of a second for tenth place. After almost three kilometres of racing, my result was one hundredth of a second behind ninth and one hundredth ahead of twelfth. The point is that you're in a perpetual search for tiny amounts of time. You have to be willing to experiment with different driving lines, different ways of adapting your equipment, most significantly relating to the rocker and cut of the runners (affecting how much grip you have on the ice), and so on. All of this is in addition to the ways in which any athlete attempts to best prepare mentally and physically for competition.

At the highest level, it's about constant experimentation. Most of the time, the experiment fails to illuminate anything of value, but we live with it and even embrace it because we've still learned *something*. It is a necessary process in which we move closer to our true potential. In my sport, and I would argue in all sports to varying degrees, there is a relationship between success and a *willingness* to fail.

In the year leading up to the Olympics in Torino, we were lucky enough to use the wind tunnel at the National Research Council in Ottawa on two separate occasions. Each time for me personally, the data only confirmed that I was already using a helmet and suit that worked best for me. The testing didn't cause me to change anything other than my saddle, a padded steel frame that holds you in place on the sled, and once the season started, it gave me really painful bruises on both thighs any time I had even a mild hit against a wall during a run. It was probably a touch better aerodynamically, but in addition to the bruising, it was unusable because of the awkward position I needed to maintain. I ended up changing back to the original design at the first opportunity. After all that experimentation and testing, I didn't make any changes that made me a faster slider. But I did gain peace of mind that I was using the correct equipment *for me*.

Something I think might be unique to the sliding sports is the fact that you need to be at a very high level of technical proficiency to know that whatever change you make is actually what makes the difference on the clock. If you alter your steering in a specific location on the track and it makes a difference of a tenth of a second by the finish line, then you've *really* got something. But you'll never know it if you're incapable of sliding two consecutive runs that are within a tenth of a second. In other words, is the change in time a reflection of the change in steering or just the inconsistency of the driving? Or because the push time or the speed when you got on the sled was different? Or because there was a change in ice temperature or a deterioration in ice quality?

This speaks to how related and intertwined all these concepts are. As a coach I always believed the best thing for the development of a new skeleton athlete was to literally spend their first few years getting really proficient on one relatively easy track. Calgary has always served this purpose well. You need that much time to begin to relax and feel those very slight changes in pressure within a corner. You also need to be a student of your sport to analyze the times and the video and to get the track so engrained in your mind that at the end of a run you can quickly and accurately recall how well you executed each segment.

Some of the greatest athletes I've known in terms of technical proficiency have had an almost photographic recall of a track. Melissa Hollingsworth occasionally made a comment about a runner mark or something completely unrelated to how you needed to steer the course that she randomly observed flying by at over 100 km/h. I've found this to be relatively common in the sliding sports, in skiing, and really with any sport in which there's an actual course. What these athletes are showing is not necessarily some superior innate mental ability. It's a reflection of how much time they've spent thinking, visualizing, and obsessing about every inch of a track such that a given run becomes a small amount of information seen within a pre-existing framework.

Dedication and becoming a student of your sport leads to self-awareness. Self-awareness then, in addition to dedication and being a student of your sport, leads to a level of proficiency that allows for much more specific and accurate testing and experimentation. This takes years, but only then do you reach the level of an elite performer. All of this is predicated on a growth mindset and the understanding that mistakes will be made every step of the way, from merely being slow, all the way up to crashes and injuries. Each incident is also on a moving scale from knowing exactly what happened to the most unnerving state of having something go dramatically wrong at high speed and *not* knowing how or why.

Failure can be frustrating and embarrassing, even catastrophic, but it is also without question *necessary*. You simply cannot hope to be an elite level competitor without it.

5. Own It

"You are not a failure until you start blaming others for your mistakes."

—John Wooden

"I hate it when I hear people talk about the conditions or their skates or their training or…there's always an excuse, right? You point that finger at anyone but yourself, you're never going to make it."

—Kristina Groves

This chapter is really an extension of the previous one, but I wanted to separate it out and give it its own space because the concept is critical to athlete development and applies equally outside the realm of sport. Simply put, successful people own their mistakes. They learn from them. As described in the previous chapter, mistakes, setbacks, and outright failures are critical for progression. However, you undercut that whole process if you fail to accept *responsibility* for them.

When that happens, most often it's just a defence mechanism and we're all guilty of it from time to time. Kristina Groves, a multiple Olympic medallist in long track speed skating recalled one moment in her career when Xiuli Wang, her coach, really drove home the point.

> It was the year before the Olympics. So this isn't that long ago. It was hard to know when to get on the ice. It was outdoors,

> there were a couple of delays, anyway I got on the ice one pair before my race. I basically had to go to the line and race and it was really bad. And I remember saying, "I don't know if we primed properly, the program might not have been right" or something. And she waits until a month later, for our debrief meeting and she said, "*You* screwed up. *You* were late. You came on the ice late, *that* is why you skated poorly, *not* the program." She got so mad. I will never *ever* do that again. I felt like such an idiot.

In my own experience, there is a very common mechanism in which people don't "own it". If you look at the three sliding sports together, Germany is the top nation. They have one of the best skeleton teams, probably the best bobsled team, and by far the best luge team in the world. In the sport of luge, much like skiing, it is perfectly legal to wax your runners (the metal blades in contact with the ice). For whatever reason, it isn't legal in bobsleigh or skeleton. A lot of German skeleton athletes began their careers in luge and so this fact coupled with their obvious proficiency has almost encouraged speculation about waxing.

German competitors consistently slide very quickly, even when appearing to make technical errors. Could I say they aren't cheating? No. However, two points need to be made. First, it's not actually illegal to use wax in training, or at least it wasn't when I competed, and so occasionally an athlete might do so to simulate the higher speeds of a race. Second, getting down the track in the quickest possible time involves finding a balance between speed and control. Athletes in each of the sliding sports have the ability to change runners or tune equipment to emphasize either aspect. Having a lot of control is easy to achieve, and the benefit is you can steer the sled exactly where you want to go. It's just slow because you dig into the ice more. To gain speed you need to dig into the ice *less,* but there's a point of diminished returns. If you sacrifice too much control, you end up skidding and hitting walls, thereby losing speed, and so it's about finding the perfect balance.

In training, for obvious reasons, competitors attempt to push their limits in the direction of speed. I found this to be a typical strategy for certain German team members. Therefore they tended to go very quickly and appear sloppy and out of control, *because they were.* And yet, over my entire competitive career, first as a bobsleigh athlete and then with skeleton as an athlete and coach, I have consistently heard athletes speculate about cheating. To my recollection, I never once saw any actual evidence for it. The bottom line is that the more time you spend thinking and talking about what other competitors might be doing beyond the scope of the rules, valid or not, the less time you focus on *your* mistakes and how *you* can be better.

There was a point in which the absurdity of this situation was highlighted. Our women's team was very good, with each member having won at least one World Cup medal at some point in their career. At the time, they were all ranked in the top five or six in the overall standings. The men were grouped together just outside the top ten, which is also very good, just not at the level of the women. If the women ever gave a second thought to what the Germans were doing, I was never aware of it. It was, however, a regular topic of conversation amongst the men.

From the outside looking in, it made no sense. How could this be an issue with the men and of no concern to the women? Were the German men cheating but not the German women? Perhaps our women were cheating but not sharing their secrets with our men's team? I believe what psychologists call "self-serving bias" comes into play, but whether it does or not, what we know for sure is that successful people focus very well on what they can control and pay little attention to what they can't. They focus on addressing their own mistakes. They *own it.*

Our women's team knew that if they focused exclusively on what they had to do, they would succeed. If they took care of *their* business, they won medals. They had no reason to suspect the people they could *beat* were cheating.

Elite sport is very rarely about knowing something the competition doesn't know. It's *always* about execution.

* * *

A few years ago now I happened to be at a local recreation facility for a workout while they were hosting a wrestling tournament. Wrestling was my sport in high school so I took some time to watch a few matches. It featured some of the top high school wrestlers in the area as well as an elite team visiting from Japan. In one particular match, the referee was forced to make a call that really could have gone either way. As per the rules of the sport at the time, the referee on the mat makes the initial call and two judges on the sidelines either agree or they don't. If at least one agrees, the call stands, and in this case they both agreed. The coach of the wrestler on the losing end of the call was immediately up in arms yelling at the referee and making a commotion as to how unfair it was, even insinuating there was some kind of conspiracy in favour of the visiting Japanese competitor.

When I started watching, the match was tied, but from the point the call was made onward, it became somewhat one-sided in favour of the visitor. This of course only spurred on the coach's complaining. For me it was an "aha" moment. Superficially, the coach was supporting his athlete with great passion. Clearly this athlete would have been better served by a coach keeping him focused on the task at hand rather than raving on and on about an *excuse.*

Because of a missed call, it's not uncommon for a referee to be blamed for a loss in complete ignorance of the rest of the match when the team or individual *failed* to score or prevent an opponent from scoring. Is there ever truly a situation in which a game came down to a single referee's call? There have certainly been games that were tied or were very close right up until the end, which then went one way or another because of an official's decision, but to imply the outcome was single-handedly determined by *one call* is disingenuous.

Ultimately these are examples of coaches and/or athletes failing to take ownership of their performances. A good coach keeps an athlete focused on what can actually make a difference. A referee's decision in any given moment is essentially beyond an athlete or coach's control.

By arguing with an official, a coach or player *might* be able to influence the officiating moving forward. This is how I've heard it justified in the past. What we know for sure however, is that focusing on a referee's decision *will* distract an athlete from what they need to do in the present moment.

* * *

Bonnie Blair Cruikshank is an iconic speed skater that I reference later in the book. I was put in contact with her originally through a mutual friend named Moira who was a teammate of Bonnie's for many years. There was one incident in particular Moira shared that wouldn't have been pleasant for her at the time, but it was a great lesson and it relates to owning your performances.

Around the time the Berlin Wall came down, it was rumoured the former East German speed skaters had been taking performance-enhancing drugs. Given the after-the-fact accounts from various swimmers and track athletes, this was entirely possible, but that's beside the point. Bonnie happened to be nearby when Moira saw her results after a 500m race. Moira made the comment that although she had finished eighth, she would have finished third if you "exclude everyone who was cheating." When Bonnie overheard the comment, she tore a strip off Moira, making it very clear the attitude was not acceptable on the US team.

Again, cheating could very well have been going on in this case, and that's a serious issue. Cheating has directly affected athletes that I have coached, and I am absolutely in favour of lifetime bans when individual athletes are caught, as well as sanctions for entire federations and/or nations when a systemic issue has been demonstrated. However, worrying about it as an individual *impedes* your ability to be your best because it distracts you from what you need to focus on. From personal experience, as a coach and even on occasion years ago being that athlete worrying and speculating about it, over all that time, *nothing has ever come of it.* It has only ever been a distraction.

Failing to *own it* happens any time you look beyond yourself to make sense of failure. When my kids were younger, they each had well-meaning baseball coaches who told them it wasn't their fault when they struck out. They didn't want them to feel bad so they blamed the umpire and told my kids it should have been called a "ball" when it was in fact a "strike". I certainly don't want my kids *protected* from failure, as if it's something you need to be protected from. More to the point, handing a kid an excuse impedes their ability to learn.

The example I often use when speaking to young hockey players is Sidney Crosby. What I've noticed is when he's on the bench he's almost always talking intently to a line-mate. I don't know specifically what's being said, but I find it very unlikely that he's discussing how unfair the refereeing is or anything else unrelated to the execution of the game. It comes back again to this simple truth: time spent on factors beyond your control is time spent away from what allows you to learn and get better.

Speaking here in the context of team sports, the focus for any elite performer relates to what they learned from the previous play and/or what they're going to do differently in the next. Sidney Crosby is clearly an elite performer.

6. Positivity as Strength

"Positive makes you stronger. Negative makes you weaker."

—Dr. Wayne Dyer

"I was once asked why I don't participate in anti-war demonstrations. I said that I will never do that, but as soon as you have a pro-peace rally, I'll be there."

—Mother Teresa

In the context of sport, positivity is an often overlooked concept. It might even be seen as counterproductive if, for example, coaches are trying to build "toughness", or at least their perception of it. Over the years, there have been more than a few high profile coaches who were overtly negative or even abusive. The question remains however, was their success because of the negative or in spite of it? In my experience, we tolerate a negative environment when we don't know any different or don't believe we have the power to change it. The prevalence of the Bobby Knight-style coach appears to be less common in recent years, but this may have as much to do with social pressure as anything else. If the goal is to learn how best to communicate with and motivate a group of athletes, or to understand how best to motivate *yourself*, it's worth the time and consideration.

The Power of Kindness by Piero Ferrucci is a good starting point in terms of understanding some of the more subtle aspects of positivity. In his words:

> It has been shown that our thoughts influence each cell in our body. Thought affects blood pressure and therefore the blood flow to every part of the body. The quality of our thoughts is felt throughout our organism. Will we make them thoughts of hatred and revenge, or love and happiness?

The chapters of his book are broken down into a number of human characteristics like *humility, trust, respect,* and *gratitude.* It's an easy read but it's not just an opinion piece. The author makes reference to specific research showing how positive people lead healthier and happier lives.

> In a famous experiment, subjects were asked to remember two experiences of betrayal, one in which they were betrayed by a parent, another by a partner. Meanwhile, they were hooked up to various stress-detector machines that checked their blood pressure, heartbeat, muscle tension in the forehead, and galvanic skin response. The findings were revealing. It was immediately evident that the people fell into two distinct categories: high and low forgivers. Not only did the low forgivers show higher measurements of stress, the high forgivers had fewer health problems and had seen their doctors less frequently. In another study, it was shown that those who forgive, besides enjoying better physical health, suffer less from anxiety and depression. Forgiveness promotes physical and mental health.

Ferrucci goes on to describe measurable relationships between various positive traits, and not just physical and mental *health,* but physical and mental *strength.* This is an important distinction in terms of overcoming the stigma that psychology (sport psychology or otherwise) is for addressing weakness, or some kind of flaw as opposed to building strength or resilience.

I remember watching television one day, randomly flipping through the channels when I came across Dr. Wayne Dyer in one of his PBS specials. I had read *The Power of Intention* and quite liked it, so I watched for a while when I heard Dr. Dyer say something that has stuck with me ever since. All he said was, "Positive makes you stronger. Negative makes you weaker." He paused in his presentation and then repeated this very key concept that I had never heard expressed in such simple terms. It struck me that I had been missing half of the equation.

On the one hand, we readily accept as fact that negative makes you weaker. We know that tension and stress and negative emotion can cause high blood pressure, ulcers, and a myriad of other health issues that can manifest over time into life-threatening illnesses like heart attack and stroke. And yet we don't acknowledge the opposite could be true as well—that positive makes you stronger. As I mentioned above, kindness, humility, and other very positive attributes are, under certain circumstances, seen as weakness. In the context of sport, we are often encouraged to be relentless, dominant, and even cruel at times. In an effort to be these things, are we in fact undermining a source of strength?

What I've noticed personally is that really successful athletes in the vast majority of cases are also very positive people. A skeptic might say that successful people are positive *because* they're successful. However, in the cases where I've known an athlete prior to them achieving their Olympic success, without exception, positive was something they had always been. In fact, they had always been essentially the same person—very positive and possessing an attitude that made them stronger.

If you want to emulate successful athletes or people, positivity is something to strive for, in your own thought process, as well as with whom you choose to surround yourself. On too many occasions for me to ignore, I've felt stronger in positive environments and weaker in negative ones. It's not something I'd be willing to compromise on at this point in my life.

* * *

In the fall of 1999, just as I made the decision to switch from bobsleigh to skeleton, I had a personal experience that illustrated the power of positivity. In fact, I believe I had a measurable, physical adaptation to the support I received from certain individuals and the overall environment of my newly adopted sport.

Prior to my transition, I was growing increasingly tired with the politics in bobsleigh at the time. It was my perception that the sport seemed to cultivate a negative atmosphere with very little sense of team. There was a lot of testosterone and bravado amongst the men, and there was certainly a sense of who was part of the "in crowd" and who was not. I wish it could have just been about pushing and driving a bobsled, but having to arrange a crew, getting competitive equipment, and just being dependent on too many other factors and people made things seem out of my control.

I also had this strange sense the coaches didn't see me as world or Olympic-level potential. My testing results were pretty good, but it seemed as though I wasn't getting the same opportunities to move up as some of my competitors. This perception was confirmed a few years later by Ivo Ferriani immediately after I had won the 2004 World Championships in skeleton. As I write this, Ivo is the current president of the international governing body for bobsleigh and skeleton, and has been since 2010. He was previously the head coach of our national federation when I originally qualified for the national team in the fall of 2000. He confided in me that he had to argue on my behalf to give me that first opportunity with the national skeleton team as there was a perception amongst the bobsleigh coaches that I didn't have *the right stuff* and was therefore not worth the investment. I guess he thought I would take the comment in the best possible light having just won a world title.

In any case, due to the negative environment as well as my (accurately) perceived limited prospects in bobsleigh, and because it looked like the International Olympic Committee would soon vote to reintroduce skeleton into the Olympic program, I decided to make the switch. I had only mentioned my decision to a few people when I ran into a guy by the name of Steve Ovis crossing a parking lot near the sliding venue in Calgary. Steve was a former national team competitor and a current administrator in skeleton, and I had known him for a while at the time so it wasn't unusual to have a conversation. However, I did find what he said to me that day *very* unusual.

He simply walked up to me and started talking, and if this isn't word for word, it's close:

> Hey Duff, I heard you're switching to skeleton. That's great! With your bobsledding background and driving ability, you'll pick it up in no time. It's just a matter of learning how to steer a different kind of sled. I think you're going to do awesome. You're going to make the national team! And to qualify for the Olympics all you have to do is finish in the top fourteen at World's, and next year World's are going to be held in

Calgary, which is your home track. You're going to go to the Olympics!

In all honesty, I was stunned. In my mind looking back, I just stood there with my mouth open while Steve talked and then walked away without me saying a word. I felt like it had been years since anyone had said anything remotely positive like that to me. I never saw myself as someone who needed external motivation, but in my athletic career, it was very unusual to have someone just come right out and say they *believed* in me and thought I would succeed. It was something I'll never forget, although in the moment, I didn't fully appreciate what a difference his words would make.

I think that brief encounter with Steve had such an effect because, in part, I perceived him as being someone who knew what he was talking about. He had been involved with the sport for years and had represented his country internationally many times. He certainly had credibility, and it made me consider the possibility he was right! That chance meeting affected how I saw the sport and my place in it. And having come from what I perceived as a very negative environment into one that was significantly more positive, there were almost immediate measurable effects. Positive *literally* made me stronger.

The best illustration of this came in the form of a sprint test within a month of my encounter with Steve. Every year in both bobsleigh and skeleton, the national team conducts physical testing in the fall which includes a 30m sprint test. My time after switching to skeleton was almost a tenth of a second faster than my previous personal best. Keep in mind I had been training for the better part of a decade at that point, to be stronger and faster.

To then knock a tenth of a second off my time in a short sprint, at thirty-three years old—that *shouldn't* happen.

My brief interaction with Steve that day has also affected me in terms of how I try to support other people, and this is not limited to athletes. Any time I see someone showing potential of some kind, or showing leadership or character, I try to make a point of telling them, regardless of whether I'm their coach, a friend, or just happen to observe them in passing. I've come to appreciate that it often takes very little effort to impact someone else in a significant way. I do this in the hope that I may have the same effect on someone else as Steve had on me all those years ago.

I don't care how confident you are or what level you have achieved. Every so often, we all need to hear that someone else, someone with a little credibility perhaps, thinks we can do it too.

* * *

With respect to coaching and/or leadership, a lot has been written about positive versus negative reinforcement, the ratio in which you should give each, and so on. The consensus is that positive comments should be given several times more frequently than negative. An aspect that is sometimes missed in the discussion is the *meaningfulness* of the feedback in the sense that if we adhere too closely to rigid schedules, it can affect whether the person receiving the feedback sees it as credible and ultimately believes it or not.

As I mentioned before, I once had a roommate who was an accomplished track cyclist. Although competing in different sports, we were both power athletes and I looked up to him. In the weight room, I had a really good squat, but his squat made mine look average. Truthfully, I was in awe of his physical abilities and the international success he had achieved. Richard was a very positive person and always had a supportive comment and sometimes even a prediction as to how successful he thought I might be in the future. For a long time, I was really excited to hear his comments until I realized that he rarely if ever said anything negative. Eventually it was less meaningful to me because it was *always* positive, regardless of my perception of what I had done to warrant it. In hindsight it seems very petty to be critical of someone for being *too* positive, but there is a balance to be struck to maintain the meaningfulness of feedback. Of course when I talk to Richard these days, he just says he was right! How can I argue with that?

For coaches, there's a time and place for listening and understanding, and there's a time for barking out commands at athletes to get them going. Even so, *meaningful positive* reinforcement remains the most powerful modifier of behaviour. My father was at one time a high school football coach. From what I understand, he did not hand out compliments easily. My sisters and I have each heard stories about the lengths to which his players would go to hear a very simple and specific phrase that carried with it a great deal of meaning.

The short article below was written by Neil Crone, a successful actor and writer, who was coached by my father so many years ago as a high school football player. Aside from being a very heartfelt tribute that still means a great deal to my family, it also illustrates the importance of meaningful praise.

> I received the news yesterday that my old football coach, and dear friend had passed away. The last time we saw each other was a little over a year ago at a high school reunion. We were

both going through chemotherapy at that time. It was a strange and for me certainly a very emotional meeting. Here was a man who over a very short period of time had an enormous impact on what kind of person I was to become. Next to my own father, I don't think I've ever come so close to idolizing another individual in my life. In those impressionable high school years, he was as good a role model as I could've chosen I think. He was highly intelligent, bitingly funny and possessed of immense power and self-confidence. I was immediately drawn to him and felt I would've done anything to win his favour.

Almost thirty years later, I can still remember one particular, chilly autumn rain soaked football practice. In the middle of a scrimmage, the ball was snapped and the quarterback faked a hand-off to the halfback who was running to the left. I noticed however, that the fullback was drifting right and the guards were pulling in the same direction. I followed, and sure enough the quarterback pitched the ball to the fullback for a power sweep to the right. I ran as hard as I could, tracking with him as he sprinted to the sidelines, looking for an opening to turn up field. He was fast and he was closing in on a gap that would leave nothing between him and the goal line. In the instant he hit that gap, I dove and after sailing through the air for what felt like twenty feet, hit him square in the side and knocked him flying out of bounds for a loss. It was, if I do say so myself, a pretty spectacular tackle.

On my knees and scraping mud off of my face-mask I noticed we had landed right at the feet of my coach. Panting, I stood up and looked at him. He just nodded and with his customary brevity said only, "Nicely done."

Two words, only two words. But never have two words meant more to a person.

Like my old football jersey, which sits in the bottom of a drawer in my bedroom and has now survived being thrown out by a mother and a wife, I have carried that "nicely done" with me ever since.

—Neil Crone

7. Embodying Team

"It is one of the most beautiful compensations of this life that you cannot sincerely try to help another without helping yourself."

—Ralph Waldo Emerson

One of the challenges of being on a team of athletes who compete in an individual sport is the fact that your teammate is also your competition. You share resources, you travel, train, and even room together with other skilled competitors who want nothing more than to be where you want to be—on top of the podium. Speaking from personal experience as both an athlete and coach, it's sometimes difficult to be in the environment and not look at a teammate as the enemy. It's easy to fall into the trap, and many have.

Of course this is a very limited perspective; everyone in your *entire sport,* in *any sport* for that matter, wants to be on top of the podium. Although I have met a few who would disagree, your opponent (teammate or not) should never be thought of as "the enemy" or someone you have contempt for. An opponent is someone who will help you reach the next level by presenting a challenge and exposing areas of your game you can improve upon.

Cal Botterill is a highly respected performance psychologist who has worked with numerous Olympians and professional teams. Here's what Cal and Tom Patrick wrote about teamwork and perspective in their book *Perspective: The Key To Life*:

> People with perspective have enough vision, gratitude and security to be open to positive rivalries and other people's needs. Positive rivalries are reflected in the sentiment "I hope you are great, because that brings out the best in me, and that's better for all of us." Top competitors seem to embrace positive rivalries and share this attitude. It is clearly a much higher level of functioning than negative rivalries and the "eye for an eye, and a tooth for a tooth" mentality that often creeps into highly competitive activity when people lose perspective. Positive rivalries bring out the best in us and promote a win-win possibility. They promote an approach-success versus avoid-failure outlook, which is much healthier and facilitates much higher levels of performance and functioning. Negative images, fears and tension are reduced and enhanced focus, connection and flow become possible.

One of the great positive rivalries Cal witnessed firsthand was that between Susan Auch and Catriona Le May Doan. At the 1998 Olympics in Nagano, Susan won her second straight silver medal in the 500m in long track speed skating, while Catriona won the first of her two consecutive gold medals in the same event. It was a case of two world-beaters on the same team, training on the same ice at the same time. Susan talked about their rivalry and you get the feeling that it was a strain at times, but the end result was nothing short of spectacular.

> Catriona and I became powerful because we were working together. I think it's a lot harder being from the same country, but obviously it's possible. I mean there were times that were really, really difficult. They were dumb things, but in the end I definitely think the two of us wouldn't have been on the

> podium without doing it the way we did. We would not have both been on the podium, maybe one of us would have, maybe the other, maybe not first. But I'm sure we both wouldn't have.

Rivalries, especially within a team, can be really challenging. It definitely takes work and an understanding of what can be gained by pushing each other. There needs to be a balance and everyone needs some down time, but if you can keep it in perspective, there's great value in seeing what another one of the world's best can do on a regular basis.

* * *

In terms of a sports resume, it doesn't get much better than Bonnie Blair Cruikshank. There have been a few who have won more medals at a single Olympics or over a career, but to win the same event in *three* consecutive Games is an extremely rare accomplishment. A few years ago, Bonnie was kind enough to let me interview her for a blog I was working on at the time. I also spoke to two of her former teammates, and it's clear she was not just a great speed skater but someone who elevated the people around her as well. Her coaches would have had very little work to do in terms of inspiring teamwork and sportsmanship, as this was simply how Bonnie and other senior members of her team conducted themselves.

In truth, when you're a five-time Olympic gold medallist, you are usually afforded certain luxuries, like your own suite at a hotel or a first class ticket when you travel, but Bonnie never went there. She traveled with her team. She stayed with her team. She never showed up late for a training camp or left early, or did anything that would set her apart from her teammates. I think they respected her a great deal for that and saw her as the very genuine person she is. If it had only been an act, they would have eventually seen through it. The bottom line is *she* didn't see herself as anything more or less than anyone else.

Something I've always been interested in is what you might call a competitive philosophy, or how an athlete sees their competition. When I asked Bonnie about this, her response was exactly in line with almost every one of the top athletes to whom I have asked this same question. There was no animosity or negative emotion directed at anyone else. Success lies predominantly in being able to perform to the best of your ability. Worrying about what anyone else is doing is a distraction.

This was Bonnie's comment about her competitive philosophy:

> I kind of looked at it as if the clock was my enemy and everybody else was on the ice but to each their own and may the best person win. And if I get beat in one race by somebody or a couple of people it isn't going to make me hate them [laughing] or despise them or make me want to kill them the next time I got on the ice. To me it was always about the clock. That's what I wanted to kill, that's what I wanted to beat.
>
> There were great friendships that you make all over the world and I think part of it is you create more of a friendly rivalry rather than a cut throat...you know, I was racing the clock! And I was racing me. *I* was my biggest competitor.

When Bonnie was still racing, the US team regularly trained in Calgary. That was a long time ago now, but to my recollection, they really seemed to be a team despite the fact that speed skating is an individual sport. I asked her about that.

> A very big part of it was we *were* a team. We traveled together all the time, sometimes under the same roof a good seven months out of the year, so we had great friendships, great teammates where we would feed off of each other.
>
> I know I wouldn't have been the skater I was, had I not had teammates like my husband [Dave Cruikshank], Dan Jansen, Nick Thometz, Dave Bestemen. I had those guys to really rely on for part of my training and helping me to be able to go speeds I wouldn't be able to go on my own. That to me was huge. And part two was to do my part to help others. You take Moira for instance, her starts weren't her strong suit so if I could be of help to her on some things and let her follow me on some of the shorter exertions to get her up to speed better, those types of things where you're helping your teammates be the best that they can be, and then when they *do* have great races you think maybe did you play a little part in it? That to me is thrilling and exciting too. Even though we were individuals we were still very much a team and have had great friendships that have lasted a lifetime.

Bonnie's drive and intensity were a huge part of her success, but it was directed at aspects of her skating and training that could make a difference. At times I found it challenging as a coach to keep athletes focused on aspects of their sport that were within their control and therefore directly relevant to their progress. From our conversation, it was clear to me that Bonnie knew this well, and she contributed greatly to a team environment that kept everyone focused where it could do the greatest good.

* * *

As part of the national men's skeleton team, I had some great teammates. Guys like Paul Boehm, Pascal Richard, Kelly Forbes, and Nathan Cicoria all contributed tremendously to my success, as I hope I did to theirs. I realize it's a cliché, but true nonetheless: I wouldn't have been the same competitor without them. To a man, they had the work ethic, and they were very highly skilled, which meant their feedback was valuable. They were a lot of fun as well, which went a long way to protecting my sanity, being on the road for weeks or even months at a time. These are the guys I worked with from the very beginning and never once felt a sense of rivalry with or jealousy of. By the end of my career, Jeff Pain was someone I could add to that list, but it was a process to get there. He did his own thing at first but we eventually pooled our resources, and the difference between the two paths was dramatic.

My relationship with Jeff was a bit of a struggle when I initially made the national team in 2000. I was the new guy, having only moved over to skeleton from bobsleigh the previous season while Jeff was already a multiple World Cup medallist. At the second race of the season in Austria, there was one particular corner I was having trouble with. We only had six training runs before the race and I was going through them quickly without making any progress. I needed to figure something out. My logic was simply that Jeff and I were teammates. I didn't know how to correctly steer through the corner and he did. So why wouldn't I just ask him?

When I brought it up, he said he had been coming to that track for seven years and up until the previous visit he had always paid his own way. They never had a coach and none of the guys worked together so he had learned to do that specific corner by sliding every chance he got, talking about it to anyone who would listen, and when he wasn't sliding, he was sitting in the snow bank adjacent to the corner, watching sled after sled go by until he figured it out. The way he put it was, "I don't think it's fair that you show up here one day and I would just give you the answer."

I couldn't argue with that; it was a valid perspective. I very likely would have felt the same way had I been in his shoes. It was my first year making the national team and Jeff was one of the top sliders in the world. Who was I to expect the answer to a question that had taken him years to figure out? The only problem of course, was that it created a terrible working environment and a rivalry began to develop. To Jeff's credit, if I ever beat him in a race, he was usually the first person to congratulate me, and I hope he'd say the same of me. It just wasn't ideal for either of us. There was a *tension.* I didn't like the fact that our relationship was overly competitive but we both played a role in that.

The turning point came after the 2003/2004 season, which was the best year of my career. I had finished second overall on the circuit and won gold at the World Championships. On the other hand, Jeff had missed the first half of the season with an ankle injury and had not had a great second half by his standards. That spring, after the season had ended, Jeff called and asked if we could meet one-on-one, which was something he did individually with each member of the men's team. In that meeting he confided in me that he had not enjoyed the past winter. He felt he had created a barrier between himself and the rest of the team and he had lost any sense of fun the sport once held for him. Ultimately he wanted to try to work together.

Individually and collectively, the rest of the team agreed. It wasn't an overnight change, and there were definitely trust issues that had to be worked through. Initially, Jeff thought we should share all information about sliding and racing except with regard to equipment, essentially because he had worked hard to design runners that he thought would give him an advantage.

After a year of trying it out and making some progress, and with only one year until the Torino Olympics, we had another meeting. This time everyone was in the room at the same time, and I don't want to overstate this, but basically we ganged up on Jeff. We put him on the spot. The discussion went back and forth a few times until, to his credit, he agreed. We would work together and share any and *all* information, including with regard to equipment, because in the end you either had your teammate's back or you didn't. Going into the Olympic season later that fall, I believe we did, all of us.

I look back on the success of that meeting and one of the reasons it worked so well for everyone was because it had nothing to do with the coaches or staff of the national team. It was just athletes. We weren't being pushed to come together as a team. It was what *we* wanted. It was confrontational in the sense that we had a division within the team in terms of opinion, but it certainly wasn't accusatory or insulting in any way. Because of Jeff's ability to see the situation for what it was, he didn't feel threatened. We came to the mutual conclusion to work together.

I think our results that year, culminating with the Torino Olympics, speak to the success of having us all working towards the same goal. Jeff was a two-time world champion by that point, and his input elevated the group. There's no question about that. But *he* benefitted as well. Very much like Susan Auch talked about her rivalry with Catriona Le May Doan, I'm sure we would not have had the end result we did without being the team we were, taking a genuine interest in each other's success, as well as our own.

The Torino Olympics were the last two runs of my skeleton career. Looking back now, my one frustration remains the fact that Paul Boehm, who finished fourth, veered sharply to the right coming out of the start groove in his first run. This is something that would be difficult to do *intentionally*, but seems to happen randomly every once in a while. It was very likely caused by a little piece of ice at the end of the groove that had not been swept out of the way after the previous competitor. Again, it's not something done intentionally or out of neglect. It just happens.

I believe this one little mishap cost Paul more time than the difference to third place. If he had had a clean start on both of his runs, we could have swept an Olympic podium for the first time in our nation's history. As it happened we had to settle for first, second, and fourth, which is a result later matched by our men's moguls skiers in 2014, led by the great Alex Bilodeau, but at least at the time of publishing, this has not yet been surpassed. Without question, we wouldn't have achieved the same level of success if we hadn't worked together the way we did. I look back on those days and that team and still see it as something really special.

8. Born of Passion

"Great dancers are not great because of their technique; they are great because of their passion."

—Martha Graham

It took me a while to settle on a title for this chapter. I thought about words like *perseverance* and *dedication* and I realized at one point I was grouping essentially the same content under the heading of *self-motivation.* In the end I came to realize all of these terms related back to hard work. If there's one thing everyone agrees on, it's the fact that hard work is a necessary component to achieving success in any field. There's a great line from Randy Pauch's *The Last Lecture* in which he explains how he became a tenured professor a year earlier than is normally required. "It's pretty simple: call me any Friday night in my office at ten o'clock and I'll tell you." The concept *is* pretty simple, but *simple* and *easy* are two different things.

In the end I chose *passion* because it is the *antecedent* of hard work. It's what makes hard work something you look forward to. Passion is also one of the few related concepts that has implications beyond what happens during the training session. Hard work takes you a long way, but it's not what makes you spend your off hours dreaming about how you might modify some seemingly insignificant aspect of your diet or equipment or recovery protocol. Passion does.

Of all the role models in my life, my father has had by far the greatest influence. Although a great athlete in his day, he retired from competition prior to my birth and so I never knew him as such. When I was very young, I did get to see him as a football coach at Sir John A. Macdonald Collegiate Institute in Scarborough, the high school I would later attend. When I think back to those practices, it was obvious he was doing something he had a great passion for, and by all accounts, a great aptitude for as well. Over the years I've come in contact with several of the players he once coached who all talked about how hard they worked, and at the same time how much they loved it.

Years later and right up until my father passed, even though we lived across the country from each other, a large portion of our time on the phone was spent talking about professional hockey or football or baseball. This wasn't surprising given the fact that sport was always on the television growing up, and any one of my sisters would tell you this was the case, like it or not. Talking with my dad about pro sports was in addition to our discussions about my involvement in sport, and very much in contrast to a conversation I once had with my eldest sister who informed me she did not care about sports and did not want to ever talk about it with me again!

Something I got from my father that actually played a significant role in my competitive success was his perspective as to where sport ranked in terms of the important things in life. I've always seen sport as something we put a great deal of time and effort into that ultimately *doesn't matter.* Any time in my life I ever competed with my father present, if I made eye contact with him, he always had a big smile on his face. I think back to when I was very young competing in judo, which was his sport, or later on in wrestling. I might have been really nervous, if not outright scared, but he knew I was fine and he projected that back to me. Later on when the pressure was at its peak at the biggest races of my career, it was just a little easier for me to remember life would go on, whether I won or lost.

My father always impressed upon me that sport was a means to an end for a young person. Respect, teamwork and sportsmanship, were lessons learned through sport, and this was the greatest role sport could play in our world—as a teacher of values. Discipline, in particular, was something he preached consistently, and he made me believe great things could be accomplished if you were simply willing to work harder. I believe it was through my father's perspective that I began to appreciate those who maybe weren't as talented but succeeded through their passion, their dedication, and sheer effort.

In an earlier chapter, I mentioned the wrestler Dan Gable. Remember his response to young wrestlers asking for advice? *Decide if being the best is really what you want to do.* How much hard work is required? So much that if you don't love it or if you actually think of it as *work,* success isn't likely. The key factor is passion, which is a quality that takes the pain and monotony out of the work. What a wrestler or rower or triathlete does on a daily basis to prepare for an Olympic Games is gruelling to be sure, but to the athletes who are contenders in these sports, they're almost addicted to the struggle.

Further to Gable's point, working very hard is a necessary *but not a sufficient* condition to achieving a goal. In any given field, at the highest level there is no one who succeeds who does not work hard. However, there will always be those who work hard who do not succeed. There's just so much more to it. Would you be willing to relocate? Would you be willing to change and not stray from a prescribed diet? Would you be willing to put off buying a home or driving a nice car because of the financial realities? This is all in addition to putting in the time and effort at every training session for years on end. To be the best in a given field, you put your life on hold in many ways. On a day-to-day basis, over the years it takes to get to the top, most people just aren't able to make the commitment.

The work is critical, but you also need to be a *student* of your sport. Are there specific training modalities that work better for you? Are there factors you can manipulate that help you better recuperate from a specific training session? How do you best modify a competitive strategy to face a given opponent? How often and how effectively do you utilize visualization? The list is endless and these are all questions you need to continually address over the months and years of a competitive career. A coach can guide you, but these are questions that are specific to the individual. It ends up being a tremendous amount of time and thought, and so again it comes back to *passion.*

Someone who personifies this idea that I've had the pleasure of getting to know over the years is Kyle Shewfelt. If you were a young gymnast in Canada prior to 2004, you may have thought an Olympic medal was out of the question. It's just too competitive going up against the gymnastic powerhouses of the world like the United States, Russia, China, and Romania. But then Kyle did it. It reminds me of a line from *The Princess Bride* when Wesley and the princess enter the dreaded fire swamp. "We'll never survive." "Nonsense. You're only saying that because no one ever has."

Like Beckie Scott did in 2002 in cross-country skiing, Kyle won Olympic gold in a sport where no one from his country had ever won a medal, of any colour, before. What's particularly beautiful about his story is that he did it at his local gymnastics club with the same coach he'd had since he was six years old! It wasn't the product of some top secret training method. It wasn't an imported coach or at the biggest and most "elite" club in the country. What was it about Kyle then that allowed his Olympic dream to come to fruition? There are of course numerous factors that need to align on both the nature and nurture side, to be competitive internationally in *anything*. But having had this discussion with Kyle, what he had that set him apart was an undeniable passion for only one thing: gymnastics.

He was absolutely obsessed with the sport growing up, watching and re-watching competitions he'd recorded on television. He terrified his parents by using household objects as if they were gymnastics apparatus and by climbing along the fence in his backyard to get to the roof, which allowed him to then launch himself from a greater height onto the trampoline. And as if that weren't enough, I read in his book, *Make It Happen*, that this stunt required clearing the telephone wires running from the back alley to the side of his house! Believing in your ability and believing success is *possible* are key components, but these are things that grow and develop along with you. Loving what you do is something more inherent. I don't know where it comes from, but it was there for Kyle as it was for so many other high performers.

The greatest athletes I have known have all been consumed by their sport. It was something they thought about all the time. One of my favourite illustrations of this came when I asked Olympic champion rower Ben Rutledge if he thought "obsessed" was an appropriate term to describe his relationship to his sport. His answer was, "Ask my girlfriend." Apparently leading up to Beijing in 2008, she had taken to waving her hand in front of his face as a means of initiating a conversation. As the Games approached, repeatedly saying his name became less and less effective.

* * *

There's been a lot written in the realm of business about the importance of finding an employee who possesses the attributes you're looking for. The psychology suggests you're not going to create a work ethic with a compensation package; you need to find someone who already has it. In the context of sport, as a coach I have on a few occasions been taken aback by the lack of work ethic of relatively high-level athletes. I'm not referring to the work done at the gym or on the track specifically, so much as to what I would call homework (studying the video, watching an opponent, mental rehearsal, etc.). My experience has always been an individual either does or does not love what they do. Almost every athlete works very hard in the training environment with a coach watching and their teammates doing the same. Not everyone then goes home and continues to daydream about how they might get better, or how they're going to become the best.

As a coach I have *not* invested a lot of energy into motivating athletes. I have had numerous in-depth conversations about the subtleties of sport with the athletes I coached, but those were a reflection of a shared passion, as opposed to an attempt to stoke the passion in someone else. At times I've been guilty of assuming athletes felt the same way I did. Certainly an athlete needs to be self-motivated to stick to a diet, to maintain a regimen of preventative physical therapy, or to do any kind of off-season training. As coaches often point out, they are only with an athlete for a few hours each day. It's entirely feasible for someone to show great discipline in the gym and then go home and eat in a manner that would negate any progress made.

With regard to the sliding sports, at the beginning of the week when competitors arrive at a new venue, it is in essence a race against time to prepare for the actual race. International rules dictate only a minimal number of official training runs need to be offered to each athlete prior to the competition. Usually that number is six, two per day over three training days. Needless to say, with the average run being approximately a minute long, a total of six minutes actually performing the sport is a very small amount. For this reason, competitors rely on other methods to prepare. Specifically, they watch other athletes, watch video of themselves and/or others, and actually walk in the track either before or after a session. All of this is for the purpose of refining what sliding sport athletes do perhaps more than anyone else, which is *visualization*. Anything you learn by studying the track and/or watching other competitors must be translated in to the context of what you, from an internal perspective, will attempt to do in the race. Six minutes of actual practice; the rest is in your head.

For one particular World Cup race, our national team arrived in Lake Placid, New York, the night before official training began. We found ourselves in a position to either have a long-awaited meal or get right over to the track to walk it once before it closed for the evening. The great benefit of a track walk is that it gives athletes the most current visual perspective. In very subtle ways, a track actually changes from year to year or even within the same competitive season. Getting in the track is an opportunity to see where the ice has built up or been cut away as compared to previous visits, which has implications for how you negotiate the course. It allows you to begin your race preparation with a fresh visual impression of the track in its current state. If we missed the track walk that evening, it would have been delayed or most likely cancelled, as the team was scheduled to lead off the early training session the next morning.

In my view, the choice to get right to the track was a "no brainer". But the excuse in one case was explained as placing a high priority on diet, as it would ultimately have an effect on health status. In another case, because our baggage had been left behind on our flight and had not yet arrived at our location, an athlete did not want to walk on the track without the proper footwear. Contrast this to an Australian athlete who was also without luggage, but when offered the chance to follow along with us to the track was willing to make the trip in sandals! This was December. As it turned out, it wasn't necessary, as she was able to borrow some boots and a jacket.

This is only my opinion, and I have no right to impose my opinion on someone else's reality, but a meal delayed by a few hours will have little or no effect on a race to be held four or five days later. A track walk, on the other hand, can be a valuable tool and a head start on your race preparation. Part of my role as a coach was to share my opinion on these things and stress the relative importance of the various components of a race.

It was also quite common back then for athletes to skip the last training run before a race to be more rested. On the surface, this might make sense, and I have to acknowledge I can't say it wasn't actually the best preparation for certain individuals. However, what I *know* is it's a significant gamble to sacrifice track time. Being slightly more rested might gain you five hundredths of a second at the start, which is a significant amount, but you then risk losing much more time in multiple locations as you work your way down a track. Six training runs is not a lot of practice. It never made any sense to me to voluntarily take five.

Early in my coaching career I didn't understand the resistance I got from certain athletes under certain circumstances. We thought much differently on the teams I competed on. My teammates and I once walked through a snow-covered farmer's field, in running shoes, to then hop a fence, which allowed us to walk a track after the facility was actually closed and locked up, but before the lights were shut off for the evening. I realize this sounds a lot like a back-in-my-day story, but we did this after driving all that day because we were consumed with getting better. We had a very strong sense of how much difference the little things could make.

The nature of skeleton is such that a very small error can knock you several positions back in the standings. There isn't anyone who wouldn't acknowledge this fact because there isn't anyone who hasn't lived it. Fewer people seem to appreciate the opposite to be true as well, especially after spending the day in a van or plane. We did. We were always looking. It was no coincidence we were the best team in the world for three consecutive years leading in to the Torino Games. I know this might come across as arrogance, but it was true. And it was true because we worked for it.

* * *

I would describe myself as an avid reader of non-fiction, and on one occasion I came across *Awake the Giant Within* by Tony Robbins. I had never read anything from him before, and he's probably the most renowned self-help author in the world, so I figured why not? In the book, Robbins talks about making the mental commitment to reach a goal. He refers to a comment we've all heard or perhaps even said at one point or another, which is, "I'd like to lose a few pounds." For people who make the commitment, there is no such thing as, "I'd *like* to". If they decide to, they do. Or as Yoda said, "Do or do not. There is no *try*."

I like to think of myself as one of those people, but I have a very good friend who has lived this philosophy much more prolifically. In 2002, when I competed at my first Olympics, Kelly Forbes watched on television. When I returned home, he told me he was taking up skeleton and it was his goal to make the national team. Prior to the next Olympics in 2006, not only had he made the national team, he also had an eleventh place finish at the World Championships under his belt, which was the Olympic qualifying standard at the time. Skeleton has a very high technical component and it's an understatement to say making a national team in less than four years is a rare accomplishment. In the end, his career was limited by a back injury. But how far he went in the sport isn't the point, it's the fact that he saw something one day on television and believed he could achieve it, and then did so, and in a shockingly brief period of time.

Flash forward, and for a number of years Kelly has been working for the NBA's San Antonio Spurs, a dream job for a coach and trainer. Early on in his time there, in a moment of frustration, he described himself as being unlike the players he worked with. He had never been a professional athlete and he worried it undermined his credibility. He referred to me as being someone with an Olympic medal and therefore, in theory at least, more credible. I pointed out that what he had achieved was much more remarkable.

He had played one year of university basketball in Canada a few decades ago and frankly was never suited to be a power athlete. I've heard track athletes and coaches say he could have been an elite middle distance runner, but of course that's a completely different genetic makeup from the explosive power needed at the start of a skeleton run. And yet, after literally watching it on TV, he decided he was going to do it at an elite level. Not being a power athlete meant he had to use every trick in the book to just get in the same ballpark athletically and then become competitive by being a great technician on the course. Being a lifelong multi-sport athlete without question was a huge asset. So which is more remarkable? The power athlete who dedicated years of training to something he was suited to and then won a race amongst people you would describe in the same way, or the middle-distance athlete who represented his country in a power sport within a few years of watching it for the first time on TV?

Since that conversation, I've actually visited Kelly in San Antonio, and it was absolutely fascinating to see behind the scenes of what is considered to be one of *the* flagship organizations for all of professional sport. Kelly had quickly progressed to the point where he now travels with the team, and I'm honestly very proud of the fact this highly respected organization has seen the value in *him.*

As his guest, I was allowed to sit in on a closed practice, which involved specific preparation for the Phoenix Suns, whom they were to face later that evening. They also ran their pre-game routine involving a shoot around with the team divided up with two players and one coach per hoop around the large training facility. They ran through a variety of shots from various locations on the court, ending with free throws through a rotation of player, player, coach, etc.

I was watching this closely because it was the only time Kelly was actually going head to head with NBA players and I knew based on our previous conversation that credibility had been a concern of his. With regard to free throws, obviously the professionals were good, but if you've ever watched the game, there's a high degree of variability throughout the league. Every player I was able to watch at practice that day missed at least once. Kelly never did. I was pretty excited for him, so after the practice, I told him how great it was that he had outperformed the players, at least in this one aspect. He told me that he hadn't actually missed a free throw in a number of weeks, but the rules were for his basket to count he had to score without letting the ball touch the rim. Two of his free throws had touched the rim that day so he had actually lost. In other words, there was a handicap system in place so the NBA players had a better chance!

In summary, my 6'1" non-power athlete friend picked up basketball in high school and played for the University of Calgary as a freshman before they hired a new head coach who cut him the following year. He never played organized basketball from that point forward, but he watched me compete in skeleton at the Salt Lake City Olympics, figured he could do it too, and within four years had not only made the national team but had met the Olympic standard. After a back injury forced him into retirement, he got into coaching, and in my opinion, deserves a great deal of credit for the gold medal won by Jon Montgomery in skeleton at the Vancouver Olympics in 2010 as Jon's strength and conditioning coach. Now he's an employee of the San Antonio Spurs where he is appreciated not just for his ability as a trainer but his *skill* in the sport of basketball.

How does that happen? It comes down to one word. *Passion.* For most of the time I've known Kelly, he's lived across a parking lot from a sports complex. Have you ever seen someone spend hours almost every day working on, not an entire sport, but *one* specific skill? That's Kelly. Elbow in, knees bent, head up, focused on the back of the rim, shoot, follow through—all as if he was in a training video, again and again, for hours. I can't count the number of times I walked into the facility and saw him by himself in the gym working on something really specific. He had fun, played around a lot and used many different training modalities, but he also spent a significant amount of time training his body to be as close to technically perfect as it could be. And now he works for an organization that appreciates the fact he can go weeks without missing a free throw.

As a brief aside, because this is a book about the mental side of sport, there were a few experts I asked to read the first draft. Cal Botterill, whom I mentioned in the previous chapter, was one of those people. He made a point relating to my use of the term "obsessed" when referring to someone demonstrating a high level of passion. In Cal's experience working with some truly elite athletes and teams, there's an important distinction to be made between *obsessed* and *possessed*. Cal also uses the terminology *driven* and *drawn*. In his words, "*Driven* is like obsession. *Drawn* can be just as motivating but doesn't have the baggage. I've had much more success with performers who were *drawn*." It's similar to the difference between *have to* and *want to* and also fits within the paradigm of being "outcome obsessed" or "staying with the process".

This relates back to Kelly in the sense that he's very clearly *drawn*. He didn't have to get to the gym, and he certainly wasn't obsessed with outcome given his competitive career in basketball had long since ended and it would be years before he was hired by the Spurs. You could argue that whether or not the shot goes through the hoop is an outcome, and I suppose it is—an outcome entirely dependent on process. Head up, elbow in, follow through. That's process. And it's just who he is, totally content to spend hours at a time on something almost anyone else would find monotonous.

There's one last *slightly* odd thing I want to mention about Kelly that speaks to the way he thinks. I was never a serious basketball player myself, but I've certainly spent my share of time in a gym shooting hoops and playing pickup. When I decide I'm done for the day, I always try to make my last shot a good one, like a fade away three-pointer. Sometimes it takes me three or four attempts but for as long as I can remember, I always tried to end on a high note—at least a swish. Kelly has always done the opposite. He ends on a miss. I had never heard of such a thing and when I asked him why, he said it's because he knows it'll stick in his mind and it'll bug him until he gets back on the court again. He *knows* he's possessed, and he uses it to his advantage.

I have to say, it seems to have worked for him.

* * *

"Why are passion and persistence key ingredients of talent? Because wrapping myelin around a big circuit requires immense energy and time. If you don't love it, you'll never work hard enough to be great."

—Daniel Coyle

As a coach I talked a lot about holding yourself to a higher standard. As much as you may love what you do, if you want to be the best at something, there are times when it's going to take a great deal of discipline. It's not just training, it's optimizing recovery, it's diet, it's physical therapy, it's a dozen other things that most people wouldn't consider *fun.* Passion takes you a long way but there's no avoiding the reality that some days it's a grind and you need to hold yourself accountable.

On the other hand, if the goal is to have fun, then great! I'm a huge advocate of sport at any level for all its benefits, both mental and physical. But if your goal is to be the best you can be, let alone the best in the world, that's a very different thing. If you don't hold yourself to a higher standard, will you be able to live with your effort when it's all said and done, knowing you could have done more, knowing you didn't achieve your true potential?

James Citrin in *The Dynamic Path* talks a lot about the phenomenon of athletes not giving their all. He points out it's actually a safety net to *not* give one hundred percent. You have a built-in excuse if you fail. As a coach I haven't experienced this too often at the national team level, although I did find it to be quite common in bobsleigh many years ago amongst those who were trying to break onto the team. Athletes almost universally want to be great, but it takes courage to put yourself out there and give it your best effort, particularly when the competition is there and watching, like they are at a selection camp.

What I have found to be critically important at all levels of sport is where the motivation comes from. Is it positive or negative? Does it come out of spite or having something to prove, or out of a genuine love of the game?

Dan Millman in *The Warrior Athlete* had this to say about the motivation to achieve a goal:

> Many people who seem like passionate individuals are simply exploiting the superficial manifestations of their vitality while living a life of reactive emotions. Such people may be withdrawn one moment and hysterical the next. True passion, like that of the infant, is focused, free, relaxed—full of feeling and unobstructed energy. The natural athlete

> generates motivation that is loving and compassionate, not merely enthusiastic or hysterical.

My interpretation of Millman's words is that motivation has to be based in the positive. It's not dramatic; it's consistent. This isn't to say that great athletes don't sometimes have drama in their lives, only that motivation to train and learn and get better needs to be steady and enduring. I agree in this regard with Millman, and this is based on my experience as both an athlete and coach. Negative emotion isn't enough to sustain the necessary drive, day after day and year after year.

Over time I've come across the biographies of several iconic athletes, each of whom could be described as having a long-term obsession (or possession). Mohammed Ali as a youngster was thought of as annoying by the other boxers in his hometown gym because he talked a lot and he simply *wouldn't leave*. He lived and breathed his sport. When he wasn't training or actually boxing, he was watching (and talking) to others who were. He was there all day and his sport consumed his every thought.

The example most Canadian kids are familiar with is that of *The Great One*. As a kid, Wayne Gretzky would skate for an hour and a half before school, do his homework after school and get back on the ice by 3:30. He'd skate until dinner, have dinner *with his skates on* and go out again until dark. Apparently he would sometimes pay another kid a little bit of money to play net. Most often alone, he would do pylon drills and just work on his skills for hours on end. You might do that a few times if you were bored, but you don't do that consistently over a number of years unless you were just that *way*. There is an unavoidable genetic component to sport as well, but being completely wrapped up in your passion is a very common characteristic of successful people —much like my friend Kelly.

* * *

Another factor relating to motivation is the clear understanding of what you want to achieve and *why*. This is not always as obvious as it sounds, and it may change over time. I'm a big believer that the first priority of youth sport should be to inspire an innate love of sport. Kids should be exposed to as many activities as possible so they might develop a variety of skills and find their passion, because truly, if they don't love it, all the talent in the world is irrelevant. We need to let kids enjoy themselves, learn, and not worry about too much else. Eventually, as a child gets older, there comes a time when they need to decide what the ultimate goal is. If it's to compete at the highest level, the focus quickly turns from "why" to "how".

As a senior national team athlete, the goals are pretty specific, and there's a reason for every action. In other words, the "how" of achieving success is mapped out in great detail. Within the sliding sports, the rule of thumb is that a great run is one third push, one third driving, and one third equipment. For each year of the Olympic quadrennial, I had a very specific plan as to how I was going to make each of these aspects, and subcategories thereof, better. It's very easy to get consumed by the details, but at the same time I never forgot *why* I was dedicating myself to skeleton. I believe this helped me to maintain my focus and make decisions in the best interest of achieving those goals.

In any sport, the Olympic dream takes you away from home, often for months at a time. That was an aspect of my sport that I didn't care for, but it served a role in terms of keeping me on track and disciplined. As with any competitor, there were times I spent training and working towards a race at the end of the week that, for whatever reason, didn't go well. For me that felt like I had *wasted* a week of my life. I wasn't there for some kind of vacation or to see the sights in some foreign mountain town. Especially towards the end of my career when my wife and I were trying to start a family, I was ready to move on to the next phase of my life. On the circuit I was very disciplined because I actually lived in fear of spending another week away from home and having nothing to show for it. I knew what that felt like, and I did whatever I could to make sure it didn't happen. It was a strong motivator for me.

In terms of the specific preparation an athlete goes through leading up to a race, it's a very personal thing. Especially in an individual sport, there's actually a lot of leeway in terms of what one does or does not do. How much time you spend watching other sliders on the track is essentially up to you. Visualization is also something you can do for hours on your own to prepare for an event, or you don't have to do it at all. Coaches are there to help fine-tune your process, but typically nobody is going to follow you around with a clipboard or ask you to account for your time. It is assumed each athlete would do what is necessary to optimally prepare.

I tended to do a great deal of visualization, partly because I was consumed with my sport and thought about it constantly, and partly because I knew what the result might be if I didn't do everything in my power to prepare. Put another way, I never had any doubt as to why I was at a track and far away from home—it was to be the best I could be. It was to make the sacrifice *worth it.*

But it wasn't all business of course. I've made some lifelong friends and had some incredible adventures. Sport has provided me the opportunity to see places I never would have otherwise. Wouldn't it be a waste to focus solely on the competitions? Especially at an Olympic Games, which is such an incredible cultural event. Shouldn't we also value the *experience*?

The answer to these questions for me is pretty straightforward. Yes! You'll have some wonderful experiences along the way and that's a valuable thing. But there's a very important distinction to be made between the result in your event and a cultural experience. To be at the top of your game requires a singular focus, an awareness and a discipline relating to everything you have the ability to control. The *experience*, on the other hand, is more or less going to take care of itself. If you're ever lucky enough to represent your country, you've put in a hell of a lot of effort to get there and you were selected for only one reason. It sounds like such an obvious thing to say, but the Olympic Games is the pinnacle of sport and those selected have an obligation to show *why* they were selected.

In the summer after the Torino Games, Visa held an event in Toronto to celebrate all the Olympic medallists from the teams they sponsored. Also in attendance were some of their Toronto-based summer-sport athletes. I was having lunch at a table with a track athlete who was hoping to qualify for Beijing, which at the time was less than two years away. She mentioned she found herself easily distracted by everything she assumed would be going on in and around the Olympic Village, so she asked a question of the group. Did we think she should get out of the Village to focus on her event or stay to get the full Olympic "experience"?

The first response she got, without any hesitation at all, was from another Olympian who suggested she stay in the Village to take it all in. I have to be honest in saying I found the response bewildering, and I had to make an effort to conceal my reaction. I realize what I'm about to say will come across as being particularly harsh, but I believe an elite performer will answer the question one way, and someone who is just happy to be there will answer it another.

I certainly don't mean to imply a medal is the sole measure of an athlete. I don't actually believe that, and I have tremendous respect for numerous athletes who never represented their country, let alone didn't win medals. Having said that, someone else who was sitting at the table was Bruny Surin, world medallist in the 100m and Olympic gold medallist from Atlanta in the 4 x 100m relay. How much time do you think he spent trying to get an Olympic experience before his events? Bruny seemed to bite his tongue when the question was asked. In my mind he's a member of a distinct group of elite performers who wouldn't see it as a valid question, at least not for themselves.

I would encourage all athletes, especially those who have reached the level of representing their nation, to think the way a champion thinks and hold themselves to that higher standard. An Olympic Games will be an incredible experience; it couldn't be otherwise. I'm very lucky in that I've been a part of many Games now, as an athlete, a coach, a commentator, and once, in Seoul, South Korea, in 1988 as part of the Olympic Youth Camp. Every time it has been an incredible event with a very different feel and atmosphere and *experience.* As an athlete I've been on both sides of what an Olympics can be. I've been on top, which meant limousine, police escort, phone call with the Prime Minister, numerous invitations to speak, and, whether justified or not, a certain credibility from that point forward, at least in a sport-related context. I've also been on the other end of the spectrum.

In Salt Lake City in 2002, I was ranked sixth in the world going in and had just won my first ever World Cup medal. I believed I had a shot at the podium, but to then finish tenth was heartbreaking. It has honestly affected the lens through which I see an Olympics now because I've felt that post-Olympic depression. You cross the finish line and walk through the media gauntlet and nobody really cares to talk to you. There's a tremendous amount of media attention leading up to the event and when you don't perform, the whole thing just up and pivots towards the next competitor in the next event. The point here isn't *poor me*, it's that you never see this from the outside looking in. You're immersed in disappointment in not performing up to your expectations, and then on top of that there's so many external signs and little reminders that you didn't achieve your goal.

Something I would never have known had I not experienced it firsthand, is if you're on the Canadian Winter Olympic team, you're *surrounded* by medallists. At the Salt Lake City Games, Canada had seventeen medals according to the final standings, which was a lot less than the United States and a lot less than the Canadian team would achieve in subsequent Olympics. In practical terms however, there were medals everywhere. *Every* curler had a medal. *Every* hockey player had a *gold* medal. Then you add the speed skaters and figure skaters and some other heroic performances and you have a lot of people walking around showing the results of their efforts. I, on the other hand, had someone ask me if I was a *coach*. I wasn't even old back then! It was not at all how I dreamed it would go.

My two Olympic experiences as a competitor were very different, but each time my level of satisfaction was a product of my performance *relative* to my expectations. In Salt Lake City, I dreamed of a medal, perhaps over-ambitiously, and was hugely disappointed. It was tough, and I felt really down for a few *months* afterward. Four years later in Torino, on the other hand, was the experience of a lifetime. I dreamed of a medal but never dared to dream it would be gold. In each case I experienced the local culture, enjoyed a number of ceremonies and events, and watched other sports where I was able to see some tremendous performances and cheer on my teammates. Overall, each experience was shaped by what I was there to do.

The reality is a great deal of time and effort goes into something that comes down to one competition, and in some events like my own, only a few moments of actual performance. It's not necessarily even a healthy thing to be so focused on only one aspect of your life for years on end, but that's what it *requires.* There are risks involved and there will only ever be one winner. Despite this, despite the fact that it truly does involve "daring greatly", if you never lose sight of *why* you're there, you have the best opportunity to achieve your greatest performance and the satisfaction of knowing you represented yourself and your nation well.

* * *

In my lifetime I've lost count of the number of times I've heard a coach say, "You've got to *want* it!" The sentiment is absolutely true. Of course a coach using an old cliché has little or no impact on whether an athlete does or does not "want it". Coaches of very young athletes in particular need to be careful about how hard they push. I would argue a coach's job is to gradually teach a young athlete that challenging yourself is a wonderfully rewarding thing. This is evident at the highest levels of elite sport where the best will always push *themselves* as hard as, or harder than, anyone else could.

The other side of the equation is, unfortunately, if someone doesn't "want it", it's very difficult, if not impossible, to get them to behave like someone who does. As a coach I can exert a great deal of energy to motivate someone at a training session, but there's nothing to prevent them from skipping therapy and having beer and ice cream for dinner if they choose to. It *has* to come from within. This is all the more reason why kids should play a variety of sports growing up. They need to discover *their* personal passion, and if they do, motivation ceases to be a problem.

Of all the reading I've done on the subject over the years, one of my favourite descriptions of passion comes from Daniel Coyle. One of the places he visited in writing *The Talent Code* was the Caribbean island of Curaçao, a place he describes as a "talent hotbed" in the sport of baseball.

> Around eight P.M. Llewellyn's cell phone rang, and I assumed it was police business. In fact, it was two of his ballplayers, who desperately needed him to settle an important bet about an obscure baseball rule. Llewellyn rendered his decision (no, the batter does not get credit for a sacrifice if the runner on second tags and goes to third), hung up, and smiled apologetically. "That happens a lot," he said.

Coyle goes on to describe all the reasons he's been called by players as a Little League coach himself, none of which had to do with the subtleties of the sacrifice fly rule. It very much reminds me of the kind of athlete I really enjoyed and appreciated coaching. You never had to motivate them, and you never wondered if they were totally committed to being their best. If anything, you needed to recommend a book or movie, just to take their mind off of their sport for a while.

9. More Than Winning

"It is not the critic who counts; not the man who points out how the strong man stumbles, or where the doer of deeds could have done them better. The credit belongs to the man who is actually in the arena, whose face is marred by dust and sweat and blood; who strives valiantly; who errs, who comes short again and again, because there is no effort without error and shortcoming; but who does actually strive to do the deeds; who knows great enthusiasms, the great devotions; who spends himself in a worthy cause; who at the best knows in the end the triumph of high achievement, and who at the worst, if he fails, at least fails while daring greatly, so that his place shall never be with those cold and timid souls who neither know victory nor defeat."

—Theodore Roosevelt

I first saw this quote a number of years ago and still seem to come across it now and then in certain circles. It is a beautifully articulated description of the value in the attempt. As a society, we worship success, and yet it may take more bravery and therefore be more *worthy* of respect to commit and challenge yourself when you are not, and may never be, the best. As Roosevelt believed, below those who fail are the critics and "those cold and timid souls who neither know victory nor defeat." The sentiment is of particular relevance in the world right now as participation wanes and criticism flourishes.

There's more to sport than just wins and losses. To use another expression I once considered too soft and too cliché, "It's not whether you win or lose but how you play the game." As a younger man, I would have rolled my eyes at such a thing, but having now spent over twenty-five years in elite sport, I appreciate that even at the highest level, perhaps *especially* at the highest level, it matters a great deal how you play the game. Drop by any sports facility in your community on any given night and you'll see examples of people who've got it backwards. As I have said many times, the athletes at the higher divisions of youth sport are often coached as if the ultimate goal was to create the world's greatest twelve-year-old. This is in spite of the evidence that factors correlating with adolescent success are of no consequence or actually *negatively* correlated with senior level success.

Independent of my own participation, and for as long as I can remember, I have been a fan of the Olympic Games. We all appreciate the great performances, but as I became more aware of the subtleties, and as I was able to see behind the scenes, I came to appreciate the great performances *within a context.* Success is relative to ability and circumstances. Through this lens I have enjoyed the triumphs we've all seen because they've become a part of Olympic history and have been celebrated. I have also been moved by equally stunning performances that were largely overlooked because they *didn't* win gold.

I am reminded of John Wooden's description of the two most successful players he ever coached at UCLA, referenced in both *They Call Me Coach* as well as in his TED talk. Conrad Burke and Doug McIntosh were never drafted into the NBA but were the two players mentioned by name as coming as close as anyone he ever coached to achieving their true potential. This relates to Wooden's personal definition of success, which has to do with the satisfaction of knowing "you made the effort to do the best of which you're capable." It's a powerful statement coming from a man considered by many to be the greatest coach of all time *of any sport,* when he talks about successful players and *doesn't* mention Bill Walton or Lewis Alcindor, who of course later changed his name to Kareem Abdul-Jabbar.

John Wooden aside, the whole focus of sport, at least as we consume it through various forms of media, is about the winners, and understandably so. The essence of competition is to determine a winner, while the personal and individual challenges faced by a given competitor, especially those who *aren't* at the top, are for the most part overlooked. When we do look closer at athletes, their circumstances and what makes them tick, it's usually in very superficial terms. During my career, I found it unnerving at how many champions were depicted as having supreme and unwavering confidence. I wondered about my own mindset as I occasionally had moments of doubt, *like every other human.* I now see those depictions of our sporting heroes as something quite different, as only one aspect of who they are, or a "snapshot" of who they are at a given moment in time.

I recently saw a short biography of Olympic champion wrestler Erica Wiebe. Visually, it was a series of clips showing Erica on the mat sparring with another wrestler. In the voiceover, she talked about the moments of feeling tremendously strong and also about how she deals with self-doubt. She talked about training and wondering if others looked at her and questioned how *she* could be an Olympic champion. Having experienced what Erica was talking about, I found it completely refreshing to hear an honest portrayal of how a person, *any* person, champion or not, has moments of outright fear about something they care a great deal about.

As consumers we are rarely (if ever) exposed to the subtleties of performance psychology. On the other hand, we are repeatedly presented the cliché that winners are simply those who work the hardest or are the toughest mentally. Certainly these are relevant factors, but remember, at the highest level, *everyone* works really hard and is mentally tough. The athlete with the greatest mental toughness isn't going to win the 100m if they're physically incapable of running elite times. It might break a tie, and certainly a lack of mental toughness has the potential to move you well down the standings, but it's not something that can replace physical ability.

The point is there are other equally relevant factors, including genetics, socio-economic opportunity, and a myriad of other circumstances that are beyond an individual's control. What we see as consumers is produced to either sell an idea, maintain the status quo, or worse, something created by someone who has never been there and simply assumes what it must be. For these reasons I believe the competitor most worthy of our respect isn't necessarily the one who finishes first. I remember quite vividly two Olympic performances that remain all-time highlights for me despite the fact they weren't wins. Both are examples of incredible tenacity and supreme effort, and in each case achieving a silver medal as opposed to "failing" to win gold.

The first was the men's short track speed skating relay final at the 1992 Winter Olympics in Albertville, France. There were other teams on the ice, but it was essentially a two-team race for gold with Canada and South Korea well out in front. That was a long time ago now and it's not possible to adequately convey the atmosphere in the arena that day, but for me this one remains the most exciting relay race I've *ever* seen in *any* sport.

If you've not familiar with the event, the relay exchange is completed by skating up behind your teammate and pushing them forward, thereby transferring your momentum in the process. One of the aspects of this race that made it so exciting was the fact that Mark Lackie, the heaviest and strongest member of the Canadian team, exchanged with Michel Daignault, the smallest and perhaps quickest. Each time they did, they opened up a two or three metre lead. And each time the South Koreans would chip away at it, so when it was Lackie's turn to skate again, they were right back on his heels.

Again and again the comfortable lead would slip away ever so slowly, until it was essentially a tie and I was left wondering if the Canadians could hold on. For almost the entire 5000m, they held off the attack. Lackie was even passed by his South Korean counterpart at one point, but then at the next exchange he launched Daignault back in front! It was incredible to watch. But in the end, it was not to be. With a few laps to go, South Korea moved in front to stay. The Canadian team gave it everything they had, and they pushed right to the finish line. The margin of victory was four *hundredths* of a second and both teams were under the previous world record.

Personally, along with millions of other people from around the world, I found it absolutely captivating. I still have never seen such a dramatic race that was so close and yet evolving for its entire duration. Canada has actually won gold in the men's and women's relay event on a number of occasions, but in my view, none of those races compare to the silver medal in Albertville. Why? Because, frankly, in 1992 they weren't the best team. South Korea broke the world record in their *heat.* The Canadians were in over their heads, and it was absolutely thrilling to see these athletes daring to push themselves where they hadn't been before, despite the ever-present risk in *that* sport specifically of crashing and finishing out of the medals entirely. I'll never forget it. And I can't be critical of it or diminish the performance only because *another* team also performed at a previously unattained level.

Another all-time highlight for me occurred in Beijing in 2008 when Simon Whitfield won the silver medal in triathlon. Whitfield had won gold in the same event in Sydney eight years prior, and that was also an incredible performance, but to me it doesn't hold the same place in my memory. I think what made the 2008 race so dramatic was that he seemed on two or three occasions, including within a kilometre of the finish line, to have been dropped by the lead group of three competitors. In fact, the commentator said *several* times that Whitfield needed to make his move *at that very moment* or would have no chance of winning a medal. Each time the group continued to pull away and I, along with anyone else watching, I'm sure, assumed he was out of the hunt. In each case, when I thought it was over, Whitfield gradually fought his way back.

There was one particular moment, very close to the finish line when I was sure he was looking at a fourth place finish. All of a sudden he threw off his hat and just went for it. It took a few hundred metres to catch the lead group and then after only being with them for a short moment, to my absolute shock, he made his move to try to *win*.

In my view, this is a key point. It was nothing short of stunning for him to catch the lead group, and yet on that day, somehow for him, it wasn't enough. To try to wait out a medal, in other words, to let it come down to a sprint in the last few metres, would have been a completely legitimate strategy, especially for someone clearly just trying to hang in there at that point. No one could fault him or question his desire if he just sat with the lead group until he was closer to the finish line, given the effort it must have taken to regain contact so late in the race. But you could argue he took his shot at the moment that gave him the best chance to win, as it was also the moment that would challenge his opponents to suffer the most.

Occasionally you hear the term "brave" associated with the pace someone sets in a timed event. The term is apt because the athlete is committing to a level of suffering that is very much beyond what the average person would ever voluntarily subject themselves to. It's also playing on a line between pushing your limits and *overstepping* them and failing miserably. The competitor who eventually won the event happened to have a little bit more in the tank, but for Whitfield it was a brilliantly run race, and watching it was an experience. In fact, I find it very unlikely I would have been any less in awe of how that race unfolded, and the performance I witnessed, had he and I not been from the same country.

It's also worth mentioning that people like Simon Whitfield aren't just brave on race day. In a sense it's easier to be brave when a championship or an Olympic medal is on the line. You know the suffering will end at the finish line and the payoff could be huge. Whitfield, and athletes like him, however, have the ability to suffer to a greater extent on race day because of the suffering they subject themselves to on a daily basis in training.

In either of these races, I won't pretend it wouldn't have been even more exciting to have won gold, because it likely would have. But these two performances in particular have stuck with me long after other gold medal or championship winning performances have faded away. They were both just so far beyond what anyone could have asked for or expected. As Vince Lombardi later amended his famous quote, "Winning isn't everything, but *wanting* to win is." It's not just about something as ultimately trivial as a finish position, so much as what it takes to get there, and then giving it everything you have.

These are two examples to highlight the difference between winning, which happens *every single time* you hold a competition, and doing something that is truly special, which is giving it more than anyone, including yourself, may have thought possible.

* * *

"To deserve success is more important than to achieve it."

—Lester B. Pearson

What is the point of sport? Why do we compete? If you ask this question to a parent who enrols their child in organized sport, it's more about wellness, socialization, values, and perhaps most of all, fun. Things change as a child gets older and at some point a decision is made whether or not to enter a competitive stream. Independent of the stream, sport *needs* to be fun. And if done well, it *is* fun. The common vernacular is "fun" or "competitive", as if it was one or the other, as if being competitive, by definition, meant it *wasn't* fun.

There is plenty of research showing just how much work it takes to reach the top level of a given skill, and that's why there are authors from so many areas—from sport to business to education to the arts—all talking about a *love* for what you do. If you apply the logic back to youth sport, it's just as important for "competitive" sport to be fun as it is for "fun" sport to be fun.

In any competitive environment, the closer you get to the top, the higher the stakes and the greater the reward for those who are successful. This often clouds why we participate in the first place. Is winning more important at the highest level of sport? Yes. Especially in professional sport, coaches and managers are hired and fired, athletes are moved to other teams or cut altogether because winning drives the finances and therefore the very viability of a team and/or league. Can we do more than give our best? No, otherwise it wouldn't be our best. Therefore, does winning ultimately have anything to do with it? Sure, but it's more accurate to say it's about *trying* to win.

The reality is there can only be one winner. If you're competing in something like a marathon with potentially thousands of other runners and you're good enough to finish, which in itself is a significant athletic accomplishment, are you going to be disappointed if you don't win? If you come second in a marathon or the Olympics or a creative writing competition for that matter, are you the first loser? There are those who would say you are, but if this were true, why would anyone compete at all?

When I speak to young hockey players, I like to ask them a trivia question. How many times did the Stanley Cup Champions lose during the regular season last year? As the NHL currently operates, games continue through overtime and then to a shootout until a winner is determined. A single point is awarded to the team who ultimately loses if it was a tie at the end of regulation time, but there is still a winner and loser of every single game. Therefore, by definition, in an 82-game schedule an *average* team wins 41 and loses 41. You might expect the Stanley Cup winners to be a lot better. It's professional sport after all, and it's *about* winning. The kids I ask are usually well off the mark in their predictions. Omitting the shortened 2019/20 and 2020/2021 seasons, here's the answer to the question over the previous six seasons:

2018/19	St. Louis Blues	37 losses
2017/18	Washington Capitals	33 losses
2016/17	Pittsburgh Penguins	32 losses
2015/16	Pittsburgh Penguins	34 losses
2014/15	Chicago Blackhawks	34 losses
2013/14	Los Angeles Kings	36 losses

Based on the guesses, people generally assume that champions lose dramatically less often than they actually do. So why is that? There are a number of factors at play here, including the parody of teams in the NHL, as well as the nature of the sport. Specifically, it's relatively common in hockey to see one team control the play and generate significantly more scoring chances but lose because of a superior goaltending performance. The point is that everybody, and every team, loses. In some sports like hockey, even the very best teams lose *all the time.* It's a part of sport at every level. What's more relevant than win or lose is the mindset. How do you react to failure? How do you learn from it to improve and/or best prepare for the next time?

Great athletes are motivated by *the challenge* and *progression*—not winning so much as *trying* to win. In timed events, this is true to the extent that many will fail dramatically trying to maintain a winning pace. You actually see it quite regularly in skiing, especially in the technical events. At the end of the first run, if you're a whole second off the lead, you might as well go for it. What have you got to lose? You see the same thing in the longer distance events in various sports. People attempt to hold the pace that will put them in the medal hunt. Some move up significantly in the standings and occasionally someone like Simon Whitfield might come from well back to get onto the podium. More often than not, however, people hit the proverbial wall or at the very least take themselves out of the running.

Is there any shame in that? Absolutely not. In fact, I'd say the opposite.

* * *

Sport, and the world at large, continues to evolve in many ways. There are certainly added challenges faced by young athletes since the advent of social media. You almost have to promote yourself in addition to all the other aspects an athlete has to manage. The human mind, however, remains as it is. When I spoke with Bonnie Blair Cruikshank, who retired in 1995, I was struck with just how poignant our conversation was. What we talked about had nothing to do with equipment, training methods, or anything that might progress over time. It had to do with the basic tenets of a competitive philosophy, which is, in a sense, timeless.

I had heard Bonnie speak previously about how the road to success came through *personal bests.* When a multiple Olympic gold medallist talks about personal bests and how they are the *real* measuring stick, it seems counterintuitive. She's won so often and so dominantly, you forget what went into making it happen. You almost assume she won every race she entered. I asked Bonnie about being the best, and her immediate response was, "I wasn't always!"

> I go back to Sarajevo, my first Olympic Games, and I only took part in the 500m and if I get anywhere near the top ten, that'd be huge. And I placed eighth! If the video would have been on me, but on American TV they only show who gets a medal [laughing], you would have thought I'd won the race

> because I was so excited for how I did at that event—way better than I had ever expected. I mean I was on top of the world! You've got to look at it relative to *you,* and the better you can be relative to you, the better you can be relative to the rest of the world. But you can't be better than the rest of the world if you can't better yourself.

Bonnie talked a lot about the 1500m race at her last Olympics. The result wasn't considered "successful" in terms of how it was perceived by the media or the general public. She sees it quite differently.

> In Lillehammer, given the three races I took part in, the 500, the 1000 and the 1500, the 1500 was my best race. It was a personal best by over a second. It was an American record, faster than I had ever gone *ever,* so to me that was like winning a gold medal even though it was fourth. Now I don't want to take away from the two gold medals that I won because those were thrilling and exciting races, but if I have to look at pure athleticism, and goals of skating there at the Games, that was my best race and I was fourth. And I was just as proud of that fourth place finish as I was of the gold medals.

At that point I asked her if she would go so far as to say it was her best race in terms of her personal satisfaction.

> Yes, yes! I look at that 1500 and that was the best I had and it was fourth and that was something that I was *really* proud of. When I was in the media room and they were throwing microphones in front of me and they were saying, "Aren't you

disappointed?" and "You just missed a bronze!" And it wasn't [disappointing for me]. I was still happy with what I did."

Bonnie Blair Cruikshank remains one of the most decorated Winter Olympians from the United States, but her dominance in the 500m and 1000m races as well as her fourth place finish in the 1500m typifies something that is true for any level athlete. Success and personal satisfaction are always relative to *expectation,* which is based on ability. Bonnie was the best in the world in the sprint events and winning gold *was* performing to the best of her ability, as was the fourth place finish in the event she wasn't quite as competitive in. The same was true of her eighth place finish in Sarajevo and during the years when she wasn't ranked high enough to represent the US internationally at all.

There are those who would insist sport is ultimately about winning gold. For a *few* people, it is. It was for Bonnie Blair at the peak of her career. But for most people, even most Olympians, it's not. It wasn't for Bonnie either for most of her career.

It's more about progress, so that down the road, maybe you get the chance to take your shot. The stepping stones to that moment are personal bests.

* * *

I want to end this very important chapter with the words of Jason Dorland. Jason was an Olympic rower who for a period of time before beginning his consulting work was a high school teacher and coach in the same sport. His first book entitled *Chariots and Horses* was about the evolution of his mindset as it relates to competition and *winning.* It's a wonderful book, by the way, and an absolutely captivating story.

I reached out to Jason about his book several years ago now, as I wanted to buy a copy for each member of the national skeleton team, which I was coaching at the time. He and I have kept in touch since then, and I've very much enjoyed our conversations over the years. Something I've found interesting is how his message is sometimes received. If, for example, one of his interviews is shown somewhere you can leave comments, it becomes obvious that people confuse what he's saying as being *against* competition. I remember reading one comment where the man had assumed Jason's intent was somehow to take the sting out of failure, stating, "[What kids] need to learn is that the world can be a harsh place, and that they might one day face disappointment." This is a completely valid perspective, but it misses the point Jason is making.

He's not advocating for *less* competitiveness. What he's talking about is actually leaning in the opposite direction. It's about aiming beyond something that is ultimately of little consequence, like the result of a high school rowing competition. As I've expressed many times before, we have a youth sport system designed as if the goal was to produce a world-class twelve-year-old. If that were the case, it would be *very* important who wins a competition between twelve-year-olds. But this kind of a system is self-defeating if we care about these athletes moving beyond their childhood.

What Jason expresses so wonderfully is a philosophy about seeing the bigger picture and striving to achieve your potential. I have found his philosophy to ring true for me on my journey, and I've included his words here because I haven't heard it put better.

> The way I coach now is to encourage my athletes to let go of the outcome and not focus on winning or *not* losing but to

> simply be present to the process and take care of all those things they can affect. If, as a result of that, you beat your competitors and win, terrific. If you don't and you still executed your best race, and you did everything that you could have, there's still something to celebrate in that.
>
> I was taught at a very young age that losing was wrong, and there was nothing to celebrate in losing. When you put the win out there as the ultimate achievement, you limit the potential of the athlete. As soon as you draw a line in the sand, you tell them what's good enough. There's *no* good enough. You're always striving to see what you're *capable* of. It's always a quiet personal challenge.

To me, that's just beautiful. "There's *no* good enough." As a coach, I can echo the sentiment. I'm not overly concerned with how *good* you are. I'm *really* excited about what you're *capable* of.

10. Finding Perspective

"You know, winning a world title is not that important in life."
—Kelly Slater, 11-Time World Champion Surfer

Years ago now, prior to the 2010 Olympics, I wrote a blog about the value of sport and how some of the greatest athletes were also great people with a healthy perspective as to where sport fits in the grand scheme of things. To this day, Clara Hughes is the only athlete in the world who's won multiple medals at both the Summer and Winter Olympics, and I asked her if she'd consider contributing to the blog. She wrote the following piece, sent it to me, and told me I should write a book. Thank you, Clara.

> I get asked about winning often. As an Olympic athlete, I learned early in my sporting life that this is what most people are interested in. After four Olympic Games, two Summer and two Winter in cycling and speed skating, respectively, I've witnessed countless performances that I consider amazing. You know what? Most of these "amazing races" do not involve winning medals.
>
> I remember being in Atlanta in my first Olympics. I was at the studio in the International Broadcast Center, waiting to do some interviews after having won my second medal of the Games. As I waited in the make-up room, I watched on a tiny television live feed from track and field. I saw Leah Pells, Canada's top middle distance runner, come forth in the 1500m. The finish was incredible and the result phenomenal.

In a sport dominated by a few African countries, Leah had done the unthinkable and broken through. I remember thinking, "if only that was a medal, what a story she would have to tell." I felt much the same, having had success in the European-dominated sport of cycling. Because I made it onto the podium, the media would allow me to tell the story of how I got there.

That's how it goes in the world of sport. Unless an athlete has what is considered good looks, without success there is no platform to tell the story.

In my second Olympics, still as a cyclist, I arrived in Australia sick with an awful case of the whooping cough. I had been ill for seven weeks and wondered what I was doing there. I was underprepared and felt simply out of shape. I wanted to hide and not have to face the races that lay ahead. In cycling, there is no hiding behind technique or judging. It's simply who is strong enough, fast enough and tough enough to prevail. And sometimes, smart enough too.

I began to feel sorry for myself and just wanted the Olympics to end so that I could go home. It's embarrassing to think of the bad attitude I had at the time.

After yet another aborted training mission, I sulked home to our out-of-Village training base a couple of hours from Sydney. I remember spending the day watching all the pre-Olympic hype and trying to recall feelings of being fit and strong. I did not even feel like an athlete.

The next morning, I woke up excited to check the internet to see how my other teammates had fared in a race back in the USA. I was a professional cyclist on an international team run out of the US. One of my younger teammates, Nicole Reinhart, was in the running to win a quarter of a million dollars if she came out on top of the last race in a five-race series. All year, the rest of us had set her up to win this series. Nicole did not make the American Olympic Team that year, but I knew her dream was as big as mine to represent her country one day at the Games.

I will never forget the moment I opened up the cycling website to the subject "tragedy in Boston." The race I refer to was in Boston, and because I was a bike racer, immediately I thought flat tire, crash or something of that nature. Never could I have imagined what I was about to read.

I sat in shock as I read that Nicole had indeed crashed in the race. She had also died. It was a freak accident in which she hit a bump in the road that was not that big, and was sent flying into a tree on the side of the road. Nicole was only about 3km from the finish line of a race she was going to win. She had just turned 24 years old.

I was numb. I started thinking about the time earlier that year when Nicole and I spent two weeks in Milwaukee. We shared a hotel room and were competing in a series of races in the area. Nicole shared with me her disappointment in not making the team that year. She had an intense hunger to one day live the ultimate dream as an athlete: to be an Olympian. I thought about how negative I was, and how ridiculously narrow my vision had turned because I was sick. I felt ashamed that I had literally given up before the race had even begun.

I vowed to myself sometime that morning that I would fight. I made the commitment to excellence and to having the best races I could, no matter how I felt, how hard it was, or how far behind I might be.

I began to see commercials on the TV about the Olympic Truce and the meaning of sportsmanship, respect for competitors and self, and ultimately what it means to be an Olympian. As the Olympics unfolded, I saw athletes quit their races, some as short as 100m, because they were not winning. I vowed to finish whatever I started, no matter what.

My first race, the road race, was 120km long. About halfway through, I was dropped from the main group. I rode around the racing circuit in the cold and rain. Lap after lap the racers I was with would quit. Each time we passed through the feed zone, where support staff waited with bottles of fluid under the protection of the cabanas which were set up, another would step off of her bike. Soon, I was alone.

Alone, and twenty minutes behind the main pack, who would fight it out for the coveted gold, silver and bronze that might make their countries proud. I will never forget riding through Centennial Park in Sydney, long after someone had won that race, through the misty green surroundings. Volunteers were already picking up fencing and cleaning up. As I rode along, a volunteer stopped what he was doing, looked over at me and yelled, "Finish with your head held high, Canada!"

I looked back at him and smiled, saying, "Yes, I will!" And along I went. I finished that race about twenty-five minutes behind the winner, in second to last place, on a day when I should have been in a hospital bed because I was so very ill. I crossed the line, weaving around the crowd of photographers gathered to get shots of the glorious winners. I smiled as much as I had four years earlier, when I won my first Olympic medal in Atlanta.

I felt on that day I lived up to the ideals of being an Olympian. I also learned the true meaning of excellence: to be the best you possibly can, and never ever give up. Reporters after the race seemed sheepish in their queries, wondering what could have gone wrong. Instead of making any excuses with illness, I stated, "That was perhaps the best race of my life. I did that for Nicole."

Four days later, I finished sixth in the time trial. Thirteen seconds out of a bronze medal position. That *still* is the best race of my life. This whole experience has made me who I am today. Would I have followed my heart and returned to speed skating right after these Olympics had this tragedy not shown me clearly how short life can be? Possibly not. Would I have gone on to win a bronze medal in the Winter Olympics in speed skating, only sixteen months after those Summer Olympics? Definitely not. And lastly, and perhaps most importantly, the greatest success I have achieved if you want to gauge success by medals, when I won the 5000m speed skating event in 2006 at the Torino Olympics, would absolutely not have happened if I had not learned the true meaning of excellence back in 2000. These lessons were learned not by winning, but by taking part, and being the best I could possibly be on the day.

I consider the Sydney Olympics, the only Games I've competed in that I did not "succeed" in winning a medal, the most valuable. I only wish this lesson did not have to come with such a great loss.

Thank you, Nicole. You will forever be a part of everything I do in sport, and in life.

—Clara Hughes

***

As I write this, Lauryn Williams (like Clara Hughes) is one of only five athletes in history to have won an Olympic medal in both the Summer and Winter Olympics. The American's first love was track, finishing second in the 100m at the Athens Olympics in 2004. She followed that up with gold in the same event at the World Championships the following year, and then a silver medal in 2007. Expectations were high going into Beijing in the summer of 2008, but in what might be the *most* competitive event in all of sport, she was forced to settle for a fourth place finish.

Amongst athletes, it's almost universally agreed upon that fourth is the worst place to finish in any given competition. To be the top competitor *not* to win a medal is a tough spot to be in. It's almost better to do worse, so you don't have to play back all the mistakes in your mind that could have made the difference. I saw an interview with Lauryn a few years after Beijing, and what she had to say really stuck with me. She described the funk she was in after the race. I don't remember it well enough to quote her word for word, but the point was essentially this: she was reliving the race and wallowing in her result over and over again for a long period of time. And then her father died.

It was just so powerful to hear her describe how the race immediately became nothing more than a brief moment in her life, like any other. In her words, "It's just eleven seconds." It was an extremely harsh reminder of the role sport plays in our world. It's exciting. It's challenging. Huge amounts of time, money, blood, sweat, and tears go into it, and yet at the end of the day, it's just sport. Those who fail to meet their expectations, as high as they may be, like those of Lauryn Williams in Beijing, suffer the heartbreak but ultimately realize there are more important things, like family.

Perhaps what's less obvious is that those who are lucky enough to achieve their dream performance also reach the same conclusion. Whether or not an Olympic medal actually translates into fame and fortune (clearly it does not in the vast majority of cases), you quickly realize you're no different than you were before. And this is the crux of the argument: because it's just sport, because it's *not* one of the most important things in life, ultimately the result is *less* important than how you make it happen.

The end result of a competition is the product of many factors, a number of which are beyond your control. One of the few things you're totally in control of is how you conduct yourself. In other words, people who don't know you often see your result as a reflection of you. It would be more accurate to say your result is a reflection of you *as well as* a number of other factors that aren't a reflection of you at all. How you conduct yourself is a reflection of you and no one else. Whatever it takes to make your dream a reality, do it in a manner in which you can be proud of.

If you could ask Lauryn Williams' father if he was proud of his daughter, despite the fact she finished fourth in the 100m in Beijing, what do you think his answer would be?

As a father, I have no doubt. And from what I saw, I think Lauryn knows too.

11. Luck and Gratitude

"You are lucky to be here. You were incalculably lucky to be born, and incredibly lucky to be brought up by a nice family that helped you get educated and encouraged you to go to Uni. Or if you were born into a horrible family, that's unlucky and you have my sympathy...but you were still lucky: lucky that you happened to be made of the sort of DNA that made the sort of brain which, when placed in a horrible childhood environment, would make decisions that meant you ended up, eventually, graduating Uni. Well done you, for dragging yourself up by the shoelaces, but you were lucky. You didn't create the bit of you that dragged you up. They're not even your shoelaces."

—Tim Minchin

"Gratitude is fertilizer for the mind, spreading connections and improving its function in nearly every realm of experience."

—Robert Emmons

Gratitude as a human emotion has a myriad of measurable physical and mental benefits. So what does it have to do with luck? Gratitude as a concept is *dependent* upon our recognition of the source of the benefits we receive as originating from *beyond ourselves.* We feel gratitude when given a gift or perhaps when shown kindness from another individual, but it's easy to forget how circumstance and luck significantly affect our lives as well.

Malcolm Gladwell once wrote about the tallest oak in the forest. "It's not just because it grew from the heartiest acorn; it is the tallest also because no other trees blocked its sunlight, the soil around it was deep and rich, no rabbit chewed through its bark as a sapling, and no lumberjack cut it down before it matured." There are a myriad of factors that contribute to success that have nothing to do with drive or determination and everything to do with circumstances beyond your control.

Luck played a role in my Olympic dream every step of the way. Moving to Calgary to take my master's degree in kinesiology also gave me access to the Olympic venues from the 1988 winter Games. I trained and competed in speed skating, bobsleigh, and eventually skeleton, in each case because I knew someone else who did the sport, I had the desire, and there was a world-class facility on my doorstep. Even after having represented my country for a number of years, my success at the Torino Olympics was in part due to the demands of that specific track.

Skeleton is a sport that could be compared to downhill skiing in the sense that every course is different and a product of the mountain it's carved into. In skiing you often hear courses referred to as being very "technical" or sometimes as favouring the "gliders". Skeleton is the same way with different competitors preferring and/or being better suited to different tracks. In my case, I'm relatively wide across the shoulders compared to most competitors. This was a liability in that a greater frontal surface area meant I wasn't particularly aerodynamic. On the other hand, being wider was an advantage when competing on the tracks that required very hard steering because you steer a skeleton by twisting it (pushing down with opposite knee and shoulder). Torino not only required extremely hard steering in several locations, it also had a relatively low top speed of around 125 km/h as opposed to well over 140 km/h at the 2010 Olympic track in Whistler. If you look at all the medals I've won on the World Cup circuit in my career, with very few exceptions, they were all on a certain type of track—very technical and not with the highest peak speeds. If the Torino track had been designed differently, I could very easily have finished out of the medals.

Now there are those who will read this and think I'm undervaluing the work I put into it over the years. I did work hard, but my suitability for skeleton, let alone to the Torino track, is no different than a basketball player being tall or a weightlifter having short levers. Was it not lucky that swimmer Ian Thorpe had size seventeen feet? Maybe we just don't think of it as luck. Maybe you'd call it fate or genetics. The point is, it's not something achieved through effort. It just *is,* and as such, you should be grateful, especially when the odds are so low in finding that perfect genetic fit.

One of my all-time favourite quotes is from Wayne Gretzky. While he was still playing, he was asked by a reporter why he always played for Canada every time he was asked. His reply: "Because someday they won't ask." I first heard the quote as I was nearing the end of my competitive career, which might be why I found it so meaningful. Gretzky is clearly someone who understands and appreciates the gifts he has been given. It was a wonderful testament to him when he retired near the end of the 1998/99 NHL season, when sports talk-radio literally spoke about nothing else for three days straight. For the vast majority of that time, they discussed the *person* as opposed to the *player.* With the exception of an interesting debate about which of his sixty-one NHL records were most likely to *never* be broken, it was just story after story about how gracious he was and accommodating to fans and journalists alike.

A personal friend witnessed this trait firsthand watching the Canadian national team play an exhibition game with the Calgary

Flames at the Saddledome. This was after he retired and when there was still a full time men's national team based in Calgary, so it would have been in the fall of 1999 or 2000. Gretzky was in attendance as a spectator and happened to be sitting in a regular seat, as opposed to a private box away from the public. Not surprisingly, there was a steady stream of fans asking for autographs the *entire* game. Without any complaint or attempt to change seats or even take a break during the intermission, he literally signed autograph after autograph for two and a half hours.

Along the same lines, my uncle, who until recently lived in Gretzky's childhood home of Brantford, Ontario, shared this story with me. When Gretzky was a junior, he was similar to Sidney Crosby or Connor McDavid in that before he played a single game in the NHL, everyone knew who he was and the records he had set. I gather his girlfriend at the time lived across the street from my uncle, and at one point he was playing hockey in the neighbour's driveway. My uncle pointed to Gretzky and said to my cousin, who would have been only five or six at the time, "You see that guy over there? You should get his autograph because some day it might be worth something." My cousin thought to herself that if one autograph might be worth something, a whole bunch of autographs might be worth a lot more! So she got an entire pad of paper and a pen and went over to him. He stopped what he was doing, sat down with her on the curb and signed *every* piece of paper in the pad.

So what's the point here? Wayne Gretzky is a really nice guy? Well, yes. But more to the point, he had (and still has) an appreciation for the physical gifts he has been given and the opportunities he's had in life. He never took for granted the fact there were literally millions of kids who tried to be like him, and would argue with their friends as to who got to pretend to *be* him in a road hockey game (including myself). He was a role model and he took that seriously by always conducting himself in a respectful manner. He was grateful for the time he played hockey, in part because he knew it was a limited time offer, and "because some day, they won't ask."

Appreciation for what we have is a matter of mindset. If you own your own home, you're in the top 5% of the richest people on the planet, and yet where do we typically focus our attention? On the houses that are nicer than our own. Some would argue that success comes from wanting to be the best and not settling for anything less. For some, this is undoubtedly true, but it's almost impossible for circumstances and luck not to also play a role.

And if you only focus on what's above you, what you've never achieved, or what you aspire to be, you run the risk of *never* appreciating what you have. Put another way, even if you're successful because you're never satisfied, the drawback is *you're never satisfied!* Even if you're one of the very few who actually achieves a lofty goal, whether that be to win an Olympic medal or play in the NHL or perhaps to be the CEO of a Fortune 500 company, there will always be someone better or richer or more successful *by some measure.*

There's a much greater potential to lead a fulfilling life if you are driven by passion. Follow your bliss. What a gift to be doing what you love to do. This is also a mindset that lets so many more people *feel* and *be* successful. I've had this conversation with Olympic speed skater Kristina Groves, and she rightly points out that to be in a position to dedicate yourself to a singular pursuit is not an option in an economic sense for the vast majority of the world's population. It's something to be grateful for.

The bottom line is we are undeniably lucky to live where and *when* we do. Human nature is such that we tend to focus on the ways in which things could have worked out better, and so there's great value in occasionally taking stock of and acknowledging all the ways in which circumstances have served you well. When you have such awareness, it feeds into a much steadier and consistent motivation, which aligns very well with "the love of the game". Enjoy the privilege while it lasts or you risk being one of those who later realizes that pursuing the goal, and not necessarily achieving it, was the greatest gift.

12. Character Development

"Character cannot be developed in ease and quiet. Only through experience of trial and suffering can the soul be strengthened, ambition inspired, and success achieved."

—Helen Keller

Mr. Little was a teacher, and for one winter my volleyball coach at Bridlewood Junior Public School when I was a student there in the late 1970s. To my recollection, he was very level-headed and never raised his voice. He also carried with him significant credibility having been a referee at the recently concluded Montreal Olympics, an event that had absolutely captured my imagination.

During one practice, as kids often do, we were arguing as to whether a ball was *in* or *out*. Mr. Little called us over and told us about a match at the Olympics in which he had been a backup referee sitting at the officials' table immediately adjacent to the court. In the match there was a rally that ended when a player spiked the ball towards the opposing team's baseline. Although very close to the line, the ball was out, but *incorrectly* called "in" by the line judge. In this moment, the player who hit the ball actually went to the referee and explained that he had hit the ball out and that the call should be reversed. A player on the opposing team, having overheard this, then stepped forward and stated that he had touched the ball on the way out, and therefore the call should stand. I don't know if Mr. Little actually said it or not, but his inference was the player who claimed to have touched the ball hadn't.

Whether he had or hadn't, the interpretation is the same. There was respect for the opponent and the game to the extent that both players were willing to step forward and give up a point they felt they hadn't earned. I don't recall if Mr. Little mentioned who the specific teams were, but we understood them to be the elite of the competition, vying for their respective place on the medal podium.

I don't remember how we did as a team that year, but I remember that story. I will *always* remember that story. Being so captivated by the Olympics and hearing a firsthand account was extremely powerful to me. I remember at the time thinking, *that is an Olympian.* It exemplifies confidence in your ability while placing character and sportsmanship ahead of all else. These athletes were the best in the world, but at the same time, there was a right and a wrong way of doing things. A lack of respect for your opponent or the rules of the game would defeat the purpose and the spirit of the Olympics themselves.

It's been over forty years now since Mr. Little shared that with us, and I still feel the story is a beautiful illustration of competition and sportsmanship at its very best.

* * *

In the winter after the Torino Olympics, I began coaching skeleton with development athletes from both Canada and Australia. In the summer of 2007, I was invited to the Australian Institute of Sport (AIS) in Canberra for a week of meetings and planning for the upcoming year. I was offering to them my opinions about their program, and in return I had an intimate look at how this world-leading organization worked. It was clear early on in my stay exactly what their philosophy was.

Australia is one of the most successful nations in the world in terms of medals won relative to their population. It might seem difficult to believe they would be more concerned with *how* their athletes represented their country than with winning, but I saw more than one example that made me believe this was the case. The first was how they talked about competing in *the Australian way*. I assume most countries have a code of conduct in one form or another, but this one clearly emphasized the importance of being a good representative of their nation, on and off the playing field, ahead of anything else.

There was a moment I remember vividly in which we were talking about wind tunnel testing. One thing I thought they did very well was involve people from a variety of roles and perspectives in any given planning session to cover all possible aspects of a topic. In this case, a sport scientist, who worked primarily with cycling, suggested using some kind of padding inside the suit to try to reduce the overall wind resistance. It was a completely innocent comment, but when I pointed out that such a practice was against the rules of the sport, the director of the program jumped in and made it very clear that if anyone was caught doing anything illegal, it wouldn't be the case that an *individual* would be removed from the program but that the *entire* program would be scrapped.

The Australian skeleton program at the time was relatively new and had a modest budget. A skeptic might say the threat would never have been issued towards a larger and more established program, and perhaps this is so. However, a few years later I heard firsthand of another situation that showed how serious the Australians were about their philosophy, regardless of the stature of a given athlete or the size of a given sport's budget.

A man by the name of Peter Davis, formerly of the AIS, was contracted by our national federation to perform a review of the organization. In the discussion following a presentation of his findings, he related Australia's supplement policy very simply as this: anything you consume other than food (supplement, vitamin, medicine, etc.) must first be approved by a team physician. According to Peter, two Olympic medallists were left off the Australian cycling team *that very year* for failing to comply with this policy. To be clear, nothing illegal or performance enhancing had been consumed. The two athletes had simply failed to get a vitamin or supplement pre-approved by the team physician prior to ingesting it, and as a consequence were left off the Australian national team.

This is a nation that appreciates the value of sport beyond winning, and they very definitely practice what they preach. Considering the dominant force Australia was and is, the AIS is clearly an organization that's about winning and, at the same time, realizes the value in sport beyond the medal count.

Or perhaps it is the case, as I believe, that successful athletes and sport organizations alike succeed *because* of their attitudes and values, not *despite* them.

* * *

A while ago now I witnessed a relatively small and yet significant show of sportsmanship. I happened to be coming into the Repsol Sport Centre in Calgary on a Saturday afternoon just as a girls' volleyball tournament was ending. I couldn't tell you if they were school or club teams but they would have been junior high or early high school age. Facility workers were taking down all the other nets and the activity was limited to one court in the main gym. It was the championship final of the tournament.

Parents were there, as were siblings and friends, to watch as the match approached its conclusion. There was loud cheering, and as is the norm in volleyball, each team came together in the middle of the court after a rally to celebrate the point and/or refocus. What really caught my attention though, were two seemingly minor details as to how the teams conducted themselves at the end of the match.

One thing they did that I had never seen before was to lie on their stomachs all in a row and bang their hands on the floor to cheer on their opponents as they received their medals. And like the players themselves, the families and supporters of the athletes also showed their appreciation for the opposing team. I also noticed something a little bit different with respect to the handshake. What I really appreciated in this case was that it wasn't just two lines walking in opposite directions with a hand held out, as if they were forced to participate in the ritual. How was it different? They were taking their time. They were talking to their opponents, and I can only speculate as to what was being said, but the point is they were actually *talking*. There was a lot of nodding, smiling, and the occasional hand placed on the opponent's elbow or shoulder.

To many, this might seem like a minor detail. There are those who would say the main thing was the handshake itself, and even if it's just a case of two teams touching hands as they walk in opposite directions, it's still a sign of respect and sportsmanship. I would agree. But this was a little more, a little more mature, a little more respectful, and a bit surprising honestly given how young the athletes were. At times like this, it's a little easier for the winning team to be gracious, but if anything, the losing team was showing a greater appreciation for the winners, and in doing so, showed their own maturity and character.

With so many examples of people forgetting the purpose of sport, it was great to see an example set by some young people who didn't. How often do volleyball skills come into play for the average adult? Not nearly as often as the qualities these two young teams were displaying in the *process* of playing volleyball. Even if a few of them eventually make it to a national or international level, the benefit of being a part of that team, learning about discipline, learning about focus, learning what it means to build character and show respect for an opponent will ultimately outweigh any physical skill they'll ever learn.

And isn't it also a whole lot more fun for everybody involved?

* * *

It's pretty easy to watch the Olympics and get caught up in all the excitement—and so we should. It's a time of celebration and recognition of the world's best. There are so many incredible stories of athletes that may or may not be from your country, that may or may not have been expected to do well, and that may *or may not* be winners of Olympic medals.

In my career I was lucky enough to compete at two Olympics, one in which I achieved my lifelong dream and one in which I got the last bit of motivation I needed to chase that final step. I finished tenth in my event in 2002, and looking back I'm reasonably pleased with the performance when put in to the context of where I was at that point in my career. At the time, however, it was somewhat less than I had hoped for. In fact, for a while I was really down about it.

As it turned out, that experience became a very powerful motivator for me and therefore a valuable part of the journey. At the same time, I can remember what it felt like to not live up to my own expectations. At every Games there are athletes feeling that same pit in the stomach I once felt when you come to realize it won't be the ending you had dreamed of. These athletes have dedicated years of their lives for one moment in time, and the possibility of having a bad day is a harsh reality of Olympic sport.

Not performing up to your expectations is one thing, but not even getting the chance is another. Just prior to the Vancouver Olympics, after a long and drawn out selection process, it looked like Brian McKeever would actually do what no winter athlete had done before, which is to represent their nation in both the Olympic and Paralympic Games in the same year. But as we saw in the men's 50km cross-country ski race, the last event of the Winter Olympic program, Brian's coach ultimately decided to go with four of his teammates who admittedly had been having all-time best performances.

Like many other people, I'm a huge fan of Brian. And not surprisingly in the hours leading up to the race, I had heard some very heartfelt sentiment supporting him, some going so far as to say the decision was wrong and should have been reversed. But what we have to remember is what was so extraordinary about this story. Brian, a legally blind skier with a condition that leaves him with only peripheral vision, had *legitimately* earned his way to Vancouver. This was never a story about giving a blind guy a break, and to have done so would have changed what was truly exciting about it in the first place.

Amateur sport is neither charity nor a popularity contest. Every one of the athletes competing was there for good reason, and the men's cross-country ski team was one of the bright spots for Canada at those Games. It was the coach's job to enter the *best* team in each event, and he chose someone else instead of Brian. Who are we to question it? I'm sure Brian was heartbroken, but he'd also be the first to tell you he neither needs nor expects any special treatment.

It's often the case that some of the great stories at an Olympics are found off the podium, and for me seeing Brian interviewed in the wake of that decision was one of those stories. It was terribly disappointing for many people, and for none more so than Brian himself, but in that moment when anyone in his situation would be filled with hurt and resentment, struggling to understand what had happened, Brian McKeever showed his character. He said he definitely respected the decision and acknowledged the other guys had been racing extremely well. And then he talked about coming to the Olympics to have great performances. He didn't say it in as many words but Brian McKeever doesn't rely on favours—he has earned everything he has achieved. You don't win NorAm races or Paralympic gold unless you are very good at what you do.

When the commentator asked him if he thought they could have informed him earlier, giving him another chance to place blame or show his anger, he didn't bite. When a version of this same question was asked more than once, almost goading him to complain, he didn't. Instead he talked about the Paralympic Games and how he'd be in the thick of some very important races in only a few weeks and how he was planning on being at his best. It struck me then that Brian was doing again what he had done all his life—having no time for self-pity. Although I've never met his father, I understand he's not one to have a son moping around the house for any reason, let alone a degenerative eye condition he also shares. It is a character trait that has undoubtedly served Brian well as an athlete.

It was an unpleasant situation in which he found himself near the end of the Vancouver Olympics, having been there preparing to represent his country, only to hear he wouldn't get to race. But it's only in our most challenging moments that we really show what we're made of, and Brian did that.

If I was able to choose for my own sons to either become Olympians or to have the character Brian McKeever showed on that day, it'd be an easy decision.

13. Self-Awareness

"Butterflies are funny. Some days they make you run to the toilet...Other days they make you laugh, and long for the fight... Figuring out your butterflies, deciphering what they say about the status of your mind and body, is the first step to making them work for you."

—Andre Agassi

An Integrated Support Team or IST is made up of all the different people who support an athlete, including coaches, administrators, psychologists, therapists, and so on. The IST as a concept is a valuable thing. In fact, it's a great step forward in terms of educating and uniting everyone around an *integrated* game plan for a given athlete. It can be very insightful to the individual service providers to have so many perspectives sitting around the same table. This is relevant in both a "big picture" as well as a day-to-day sense.

An example of how this might work would be a therapist discussing the progress of an injury, which of course has implications to all other aspects of an athlete's training, in obvious ways and also relating to an athlete's state of mind. The insight gained is particularly valuable in light of the fact that almost everyone around an athlete, regardless of specialty, has expertise that overlaps with other members. It's very easy to undermine another service provider if you step out of your lane, intentionally or not. In my opinion this happens most frequently relating to sport psychology, but if you have the psychologist present within the IST, it's much easier for everyone to stay on the same page.

During the competitive season, an IST will try to meet at least once per week in terms of a formal meeting, typically behind closed doors without the athlete present. This enables some very frank discussion, which is necessary at times. It is then up to the coach and in some cases the individual service providers to determine how much of the discussion then gets back to the athlete. So, as was always the case, the role of the coach is of paramount importance.

The one limitation, or *potential* limitation, to the process is that it isn't great at promoting what is perhaps the most under-appreciated aspect of an athlete's ability to perform at the highest level: self-awareness. During an IST meeting, valuable information is being generated, interpreted, and an action plan decided upon, sometimes without the athlete's direct input or even their complete understanding. The individual service providers need to speak in an atmosphere in which they can be completely candid and having the athlete present in some cases would make that impossible. But if the athlete were present, they would gain from hearing the unfiltered remarks in the sense that it would contribute to a better understanding of themselves.

So how is self-awareness beneficial? This is not an exhaustive list, but here is the concept broken down into a few subcategories:

1. Self-awareness in a physical sense in the learning and/or performance of a skill.
2. Self-awareness of health or injury status.
3. Self-awareness of the reaction to stress or pressure.

I talk about dealing with pressure in another chapter so I'll refer to the first two parts in more depth here, although all three are really about listening for and being aware of the signals your body and mind are constantly sending you about your state of being.

In the performance of a skill, before you can engrain a movement into muscle memory, you need to know exactly what you did and what it felt like internally so you can begin to make corrections in subsequent attempts. Sports like rowing and track occur in relatively stable environments and so these physical skills eventually become engrained and self-awareness becomes less important in relative terms, at least in this sense of the concept. On the other end of the scale you have acrobatic sports and/or sports with very dynamic environments in the sense that a competitor depends on self-awareness (sometimes referred to as body awareness) to make adjustments in *real time* in the performance of the skill. In simpler terms, if you are unaware of exactly what happened, it makes correcting an error very difficult. Video analysis can be done after the fact, but ultimately this is only a tool to boost self-awareness.

I once had a candid conversation with a top performance psychologist whose name I'll withhold to protect confidentiality. She described the realization she came to working with a top swimmer who had won medals at the world level but had, to that point, failed to replicate the performance at the Olympics. Especially in the sprint events, races are won and lost by the tiniest fractions of a second, so they were breaking down this athlete's best performance into very small component parts. In one of the first sessions with this elite competitor, she asked him a question relating to the moment before the gun sounded. She asked him specifically about his breathing. Was it paused? Were his lungs full of air or partially full? Amazingly, *he didn't know*. Her conclusion was that he could not replicate his greatest performance because he was unaware of how he did it.

Self-awareness doesn't appear overnight and it doesn't develop unintentionally. Without it, you can sometimes hit a home run, but replicating the performance or performing consistently at the highest level becomes extremely difficult.

* * *

Prior to the 2010 Olympic Games at a pre-season training camp in Whistler, some of the other skeleton coaches and I had a discussion about a concern we shared. With so much video analysis available in multiple locations, run after run, we worried the athletes would focus too much on what a run *looks like* on video versus what it feels like to actually perform. At one point, video of the entire course was on a delayed loop at the finish dock such that athletes could complete a training run, collect their gear and move over to a monitor to view the run they had just finished. The idea had always been "more is better", and being the host nation of the upcoming Winter Olympics made financial support forthcoming, which made it possible to get the extra video feedback. I believe for the top athletes more and more video was beneficial, but for the development athletes, I worried it was actually a detriment. Our concern related to the translation of video analysis into what the athlete would actually do differently on subsequent runs.

Traditionally in the sliding sports, athletes and coaches spend hours after each session watching video, in addition to all the other things you do in terms of preparation and training (not to mention eating and sleeping). It can all be very tiring, and sometimes you find athletes (or yourself) just going through the motions. To help streamline the process, steps have been taken to get video feedback to the athletes as quickly as possible, which is great because they can then make corrections between training runs and not hours after the fact.

Watching a video, ideally right after a run, allows an athlete to see exactly what happened in the location the video was taken. It's one thing to identify a mistake and another step to then determine the appropriate correction. For example, if you have video in a particular corner showing an athlete coming into view on too high a line, resulting in a skid or a wall tap coming out of the corner, then you've identified a mistake. The correction of the mistake is something that needs to be decided upon and it may involve changing something not visible to the camera. It's a further step to then translate the correction into what the athlete will actually do on the sled on the next run.

You spend a lot of time watching video, which is an external perspective, when the only way you can experience or execute a run is in the first person. You need to imagine and practice what it looks and *feels* like as if you were actually doing it. After all, the point isn't to make the video look good, it's to get down the track faster. When is it too much video? When it interferes with your remembering of, or your assessment of, the run that just happened, or when it begins to interfere with your first person visualization in preparation for the next run.

An athlete's ability to effectively steer a skeleton sled is often, but not always, based on the sense of sight. There are times, however, when you have five or six g's preventing you from looking up at all. There are even a few specific corners around the world where even the strongest athletes are unable to prevent their helmets from making contact with the ice. I remember vividly the very first time I watched skeleton in Calgary. I was standing in the big "kreisel" turn, and as the sled went by there was an accompanying loud scraping sound. After the slider had left my field of vision, I asked the guy next to me, "Was that his face scraping on the ice we were listening to?" Yes. Yes it was.

If you cannot see where you're intending to go, feel for the ice (i.e. body awareness) becomes the only way to accurately and consistently navigate the track. High g-force or not, steering optimally is a very subtle thing. Does the sled skid underneath you almost unnoticeably as you enter or exit a corner? In the highest pressure corners, is the sled turning and therefore grinding the ice underneath it, or is the sled going parallel (i.e. not turning) through the pressure, which is much more efficient? And can you feel the pressure drop very slightly in the middle of a corner, thereby telling you the radius of the corner has lengthened? This is a result of a physical characteristic of a corner, which of course won't change. Therefore, if you feel the drop you know exactly where you are, making it possible to time the steering perfectly. The best competitors are very aware of what they're feeling and can react to it *as it happens.*

The athletes I coached were probably tired of me saying it, but my catch phrase was, "There should be nothing a video or a time sheet can tell you that you didn't already know by feel." This is admittedly an exaggeration, and I would never imply that video analysis is not a very valuable tool, because it truly is. But it has to be used in the context of gaining a better *internal* understanding of what's going on in the performance of the skill.

Keeping with sliding for a moment, it's interesting to look at how most of the great German teams over the years have set up their training, relating to video and coaches' feedback. Typically they would have people filming in a few locations and they would analyze the video after the fact. The top coaches, however, wouldn't video at all; instead, they would take notes. The beauty of this system is that the athlete would then talk to the coach between runs and the whole conversation would stay in the realm of what the athlete was doing in the first person. The coach would ask the athlete about the specific corner and both together would determine if corrections were needed, all the while speaking and thinking from the perspective of actually driving the sled. In other words, the athlete never had to see the external perspective on video, which would need to be interpreted and translated back into the first person. It's a much more efficient process that relies upon—and therefore develops—the athlete's sense of self-awareness, which is so critical to the sport.

It also allows more time and therefore a greater focus on visualization, which ties directly to how the athlete will be evaluated in the only way it matters—in the *execution* of the run.

* * *

There was a significant moment in my career when I realized my own self-awareness for the skeleton track, and specifically the pressure changes and the timing of it, was better than any other kind of feedback. I was training for a World Cup race in Nagano, Japan, and it was the first time I had ever been there. Corner ten is a high-pressure right hand turn where the track switches from a steep downhill to going briefly back uphill. You have to time it correctly and steer with a lot of force to keep yourself from getting pushed hard into the right wall coming out of the curve.

As it happened, I had hit the right wall pretty hard for probably the second or third time in a row. After the run, on the radio, my coach insisted I was initiating a particular steer too late. When I informed him I had actually steered earlier than where he described, he was really upset that I was questioning his judgement, to the extent that he asked me if I wanted to talk to some of the other coaches who were sitting there watching with him! So I accepted the possibility he was right and adjusted my steering according to his direction. As it turned out, I had steered exactly where I thought I had, and his instructions to back it up caused me to steer up when the pressure was still trying to push me up in the corner. As a result I ended up hitting the right wall about twice as hard as I had previously because I was coming down from about twice the height.

A skeleton sled has steel bumpers on each side that take most of the impact when you hit a wall. However, in locations where most of *the field* hits in the same spot, as in the exit of corner ten in Nagano, the repeated bumper hits actually dig a hole in the ice such that the bumper goes into the hole and your arm and shoulder take the brunt of the impact. I didn't injure myself seriously on that occasion but it was sure painful when it happened, and I was pretty sore for a few days.

The lesson learned stuck with me through to the end of my career. I had great self-awareness, and in this case specifically, I had the perfect sense of where I was, and a better sense than someone sitting trackside as I flew past at over 100 km/h. This awareness didn't appear overnight so much as develop slowly over time as it pertained to a skeleton run. I made a deal with myself at that moment that I wouldn't trust an external perspective ahead of my own from that point forward. The philosophy served me very well through to the end of my competitive career.

* * *

I realize this may all sound a bit specific to skeleton, but the same concept applies to all sports or physical skills. With regard to video analysis (an external perspective), the challenge lies in terms of putting it back into the only vantage point from which an athlete can perform a skill. Sprinters, for example, spend a lot of time looking at the angle of the torso, because it affects the range of motion and therefore the strength of certain muscles integral to generating speed, namely the hip flexors. If an athlete simply arches the back to change the angle of the torso, it misses the mark, but to an untrained eye, the issue may appear to be solved on video. An athlete needs to *feel* the difference. The analysis is not for the purpose of making the video *look* better.

In truth, I have to acknowledge there are a few very successful athletes who have what can only be described as *poor* self-awareness. I have known some who might fit in this category because they leave almost every decision up to the coach, or they've been taught to do so. I've had limited experience coaching this kind of athlete, but I know in one particular case, she found me frustrating at times, turning every question she had for me back to her. "How much do you think I should raise the weight for my next set?" "How much do *you* think you should raise the weight for your next set?"

In my view, relying too heavily on a coach to make every decision will never be an optimal scenario. The best preparation (physical, mental, emotional, spiritual) is exactly specific to the individual. Therefore, the coach is entirely dependent upon information *from the athlete.* The athlete will always have first access and a more thorough understanding of that information. As brilliant as some coaches are, I firmly believe there will never be a coach that can know *you* better than *you,* or at least your *potential* to know you.

You will always be the first one aware of a tightening muscle. *You* have the best chance to distinguish between fatigue that is appropriate to a training load and the lack of energy associated with overtraining. We've all experienced the first moment you can tell a sickness is coming on, whether that's a fever or a tickle in the throat. Could someone else have alerted you sooner? There are certain lab tests that might predict an issue coming on, but how viable is that on a consistent basis? The reality is, great self-awareness is what *prevents* issues and allows a great athlete to progress and perform optimally in a hundred different ways, whether there's a lab test or not. Even if a great therapist has their hands on an athlete every single day, a self-aware athlete is aware every waking moment.

You are your own best source of information. Your body and mind are sending you signals continuously, even in your dreams. It requires some practice, but all you need to do is learn how to listen.

* * *

As a side note, I want to comment on the trend I've noticed in recent years with more and more athletes using music to prepare for training and competition. It's especially obvious with the popularity of headphones that completely cover the ears, but it is without question more common now than even ten years ago.

There was a time when I competed in rowing, in which I also regularly used music to get myself "up", specifically for high intensity anaerobic threshold (or above) training. It made sense to me then because of what it was specifically designed to help with, which was to get the blood flowing, get the muscles warmed up and prepare for a sustained high intensity exertion. When I switched to bobsleigh and then skeleton many years later, a few things were different. One difference, of course, was the fact that I was much older and needed to be more careful in terms of my recovery and physical therapy regimen. Perhaps more significantly, the demands of the sport were on the other end of the scale in terms of the energy systems.

Skeleton is a power sport involving only the anaerobic-alactic system with the push at the start requiring a sustained maximal effort of typically about five or six seconds only. The muscles certainly need to be warmed up, but perhaps the single most important aspect of the preparation is to prime the nervous system to exert the highest possible forces in the process of accelerating the sled. As an older athlete in a power sport, I would never consider listening to music during the warm up because I needed my head to be clear and quiet. I needed to listen to my body.

If I had any issues, like a tightness or a soreness in a particular location, I needed to be aware of it and deal with it, either by myself or with the help of our team's therapist. In preparation for a race, I also needed to prime my nervous system for a maximal effort at a specific moment in time. Because I've always understood the value of self-awareness, I had developed the ability to plan very accurately for that specific moment, based on trial and error to a large extent, but also based on bio-feedback. That skill took me years to perfect and it's specific to me, and it's only possible with a quiet mind tuned into my physical state of being. Listening to music would interfere with the process.

Having said that, there's certainly more to the sport than just the start. The great challenge of each of the sliding sports is to be as dynamic and explosive as possible and then completely shut that off, relax, and do something that requires precision and timing while sliding at high speeds and under high g-forces. These two demands of the sport are completely juxtaposed and both require specific preparation. If someone finds music helps to put them in the right state of mind to do both of these things sequentially, then that's valuable. It's not my place to impose what works for me on another athlete, and you could certainly argue it takes self-awareness to know a certain kind of music will prepare you optimally for what you're about to do.

The bottom line is this: self-awareness is key to achieving elite-level success. Become a student of your sport and of what allows *you* specifically to improve and/or prepare for competition. That's not something even the greatest coach or therapist can tell you without *your* input. Listen to what your body and mind are telling you and learn from it. When competitions are won and lost by the tiniest of margins, this is what's required. It's what elite performers do.

* * *

When I competed prior to 2006, we didn't have an IST, and one year we didn't even have a technical/sliding coach. We had a very good team leader, a woman by the name of Teresa Hlady, whom I personally found invaluable. We also had great therapists, but in terms of an on-ice technical coach, we just couldn't find someone to fit the bill after the previous coach left for other opportunities. What many people would find surprising is the fact it was actually a very successful year overall for our team, and for me personally it was my best ever in terms of my overall world ranking and World Championships result.

The only reason it worked was because my teammates and I each had very developed self-awareness. We didn't have a technical coach but we learned the tracks as well or better than we otherwise would have because we coached each other. At the time there were four of us on the men's team, so in effect each of us had three other coaches—coaches who each had valuable feedback relating to every corner on the track, not just where they happened to be standing or filming as we came sliding by.

Every week at a new track we had a routine. We did our initial preparation individually based on our own notes from previous visits to the site. Then after the first training run we would meet to discuss our issues. If someone had a problem steering effectively through a given corner, there was a passing along of information. Occasionally there would be corners we all had trouble with, and in these circumstances, we would come up with a plan in which each of us would try a different strategy and then meet again after the run to determine what we had learned.

On one occasion, during our first visit to the track that would soon host the Torino Games, we were trying to brainstorm a strategy for steering in corner seventeen. We each had what we thought was a good plan when my teammate Kelly seemed to randomly conclude that it was some kind of trick. You really had to steer it hard all the way around, which typically isn't optimal, but Kelly thought he had solved the puzzle and announced to the rest of our team that he was going to not steer at all!

"Do nothing?" we asked.

"That's right," said Kelly. "Do nothing."

The first three members of our team got to the bottom of the track with varying degrees of success, and hopped on the truck to take us back to the top. When the truck is full, it drives up to the start area and so we didn't see Kelly until about fifteen minutes later when he walked back into the change room with one of his sleeves all but torn off his training suit.

"Don't do nothing," was all he said.

Sharing information was a very effective strategy for us only because we were each very self-aware with respect to where we were in a corner, when we were initiating steering, as well as how hard and for how long. In a sport where you can be more upside down than right side up, going well over 120 km/h typically and under several g's, that's not always easy to do. It worked because we could accurately convey information about a corner, and because we were willing to invest in one another's success. Each athlete's information went out to the team, while the information from three teammates came back, which both speaks to the team environment we had and the importance of being self-aware.

As a coach, I had the same experience in the sense that the top athletes were all very aware of exactly where they were at every moment coming down a track. After a training run, I encouraged self-awareness by sometimes saying to the athlete, "I watched you in corner _. If you were the coach, what advice would you give yourself right now?" The athlete would then have to communicate back to me exactly how the corner went for them and then indicate what, if anything, they should then do differently the next time. In this manner, the athlete builds the skill to then coach themselves in *every* corner as opposed to only in the few locations in which there was a coach or video camera present.

Through self-awareness an athlete will always be better prepared with regard to learning and error correction. A self-aware athlete is also ahead of the curve with regard to their own injury status or level of fatigue as it relates to the danger of overtraining and/or becoming sick. Athletes may differ in this ability, but it's something that should always be worked on by consistently encouraging regular and thorough mental rehearsal, and in general terms to simply take time to quietly listen to body and mind.

* * *

When my eldest son was still in Little League, their team got invited to a cabin outside of Calgary owned by former Red Sox pitcher Chris Reitsma. Chris's nephew Ty was on the team and his brother-in-law Layne was the coach, so we had a team party out on the property where Chris had cleared some land and actually built his own Wiffle ball stadium. It was a small-scale replica of Fenway Park, including a green monster with bleachers on top in left field. We played some ball and had a potluck dinner. The kids and parents all had a wonderful time.

What really sticks with me about that day with respect to the Wiffle ball specifically, was the enthusiasm and focus the kids had at the plate. Wiffle ball is a little different in that it's a light, plastic ball with holes in it, so when you pitch, whatever movement you put on the ball is greatly exaggerated. You can't throw as fast, but you can make it curve or rise or do almost anything. And the pitcher just moves closer to the plate so the batter has about the same amount of time to swing as if it was an actual baseball thrown from farther back. It's very challenging but it's also really fun.

At the beginning, while they were waiting for the last few families to arrive, coach Layne was pitching while everyone else took turns at bat. It was great to watch because they were *so* into it! The kids were completely locked into the pitch, and they put such effort into the swing! After their turn, they would run to get in line again, and even try to bud on each other to get back to the plate sooner. They were having the time of their lives. It's what I would refer to as a *heightened* experience of batting. You might also say they were playing *fearlessly* in the sense they were focused entirely on hitting the ball as hard as they could, with *no* fear of striking out. This was evident in the fact that they ran to get back in line again whether they crushed it or struck out.

Flash forward to the following summer when a number of those same players represented Canada at the Cal Ripken tournament in Branson, Missouri. It was really a *select* team, mostly from the Calgary area, but they got to wear the maple leaf and it was a wonderful experience for them. They competed against teams from around the world and had exhibition games with teams from across the United States. The class of the tournament was a stunningly good team from Japan who fortunately (or unfortunately depending on your perspective) were in the other pool. My son's team did play Mexico, who ended up winning the silver medal of the international division. The Mexican pitcher looked like he could have been a college player, and gave up only three hits in the game. It was very likely the first time some of the boys felt intimidated by an opponent, and by all accounts the team did not play up to their potential.

In a conversation with my son, I reminded him about the Wiffle ball game from the previous summer. I asked him what it was about that game that put him and his teammates in such an optimal state of readiness at the plate. What was it about the environment, or more importantly *his mindset*, that elevated him to compete the way he did? For most people there's not a simple answer to this question because it's not something they've ever thought about before or have been *asked* to think about. But this is exactly what you need to consider if you hope to replicate the performance.

It's a tremendous benefit to have had a heightened experience. Once you've felt it, you need to analyze it, break it down and understand it as much as possible. In that peak moment, what were you thinking about? Where was your focus? Were you watching the pitcher's arm or hand? How much nervous energy did you feel? Were you relaxed in your shoulders? How did it feel in your legs? In your lungs? Were they full of air? Partly full? The better you understand it, the better your chances of replicating it, even when the environment isn't consistent or optimal.

The example I use here is a kid's baseball team, largely because there was such an obvious difference between the two environments and the players' reaction to it. But make no mistake, gaining self-awareness is a difficult and ongoing process. It will take years and years to get there but achieving a thorough awareness of your body and mind is the *very essence* of high performance.

14. Under Pressure

"Pressure is not always a bad thing. There will be pressure—it's better to acknowledge it exists. Welcome pressure and then you can overcome it and be stronger."

—Catriona Le May Doan

"There would be no triumph in success if there had been no hazard in failure."

—Cardinal Newman

I have always found it strange when someone claims that elite sport is ninety percent mental. How can that be? If it's ninety percent mental, why couldn't someone with average physical ability come in and dominate if they were superior mentally? I remember watching an interview in which Donovan Bailey talked about the "mind games" he played with his competitors leading up to the 100m final in Atlanta. He talked about it as if he had somehow beaten the competition before the actual race, when in my opinion it was more about what he did *in* the race. It took a world record to win that day.

Over time I've come to appreciate why many world-leading athletes put so much stock in the mental side of sport. One of the great challenges of an Olympic Games is the fact that it is essentially impossible to simulate, which makes it very difficult to prepare for. And in my opinion (*opinion* because it would be almost impossible to prove), when athletes fail to meet their performance expectations at an Olympics, the mental aspect, and specifically dealing with the pressure, is very often the culprit.

A colleague of mine by the name of Frank van den Berg, former international bobsleigh athlete and now mental performance consultant, puts it best. He doesn't think of it as ninety percent mental. In his words, "It's actually one hundred percent mental. It's also one hundred percent physical, one hundred percent about strategy, tactics, nutrition, and everything else." Frank makes the point that you can't afford to have any weaknesses if you want to compete with the world's best. It's about optimizing your potential in an environment where you can be sure your competition is working extremely hard and focusing on every aspect of their performance as well. The Olympic environment and the pressure to perform deserve special attention. This truth is evident in the fact that national, Olympic and professional teams alike are investing in quality sport psychology like never before.

Leading up to the 2010 Winter Olympics in Vancouver, I happened to see an episode of a program called *The Reporters.* On this day they were referring to a comment alpine skier Erik Guay had made relating to the fact Olympic organizers were calling for an overall first place finish for Canada. Guay had pointed out how medal predictions only add pressure to athletes and one of the reporters seemed quite irked by the comment. His advice for Guay was, "You better be prepared for pressure, or get out." This made me realize that most people, including the media, would have no idea what kind of environment this world-leading athlete was about to face.

To use hockey as a reference point, how many mistakes would an elite player make over a seven game playoff series? Even the best players on the best teams get caught out of position, fail to clear the puck out of their zone or flub a pass. Erik Guay, on the other hand, has a few minutes, once every four years in which he essentially has to be perfect. This is not remotely exaggerating the truth. With skiing especially, the fact is it's just too easy to make a mistake.

For me, the ultimate example of this truth was the first heat of the men's slalom event at the Torino Olympics. Athlete after athlete missed gates, crashed or took themselves out of the running in one way or another. By the end of the first run, twenty-nine athletes either did not finish or were disqualified, including the Italian World Cup leader, Giorgio Rocca. Rocca was given the honour of reading the Athlete's Oath in his native Italy and had won *five consecutive* World Cup slalom races that season leading up to the Games, only to straddle the second gate out of the start. Watching this man's Olympic dream end literally four seconds after it began was heartbreaking.

There are also factors unique to outdoor sports. Obviously it's not possible to control the weather, so on a regular basis you have ski races that without question would have been *won by another competitor* if it had rained or snowed or the wind had picked up at a *different* time. Races are postponed only if athlete safety is at risk. If the conditions are merely *unfair* because of a change in temperature or because it starts or stops snowing, the race goes on. This is just the reality of outdoor sports, exacerbated by the fact that skiers go one at a time, so there could be a gap of an hour or more separating the start time between two competitors.

So all of this, in addition to the thousands of spectators at the venue and the millions of people watching on television all around the world, creates an amazing environment, but at the same time a very unique and challenging one. It's also important to remember that for many, the stress has taken its toll well before the competition itself. Knowing you have a shot at a medal once every four years, if at all, weighs on the mind in the days, if not years, leading up to the event. If it's your first Olympics, it's very difficult not to be a little wide-eyed with everything going on around you. More than a few athletes have found their nervous system shot by the time their event rolls around.

An athlete like Erik Guay, who now at the end of his career has two World Championship *gold* medals, is experienced at dealing with pressure. But like it or not, almost every reporter he spoke to for literally *years* leading up to Vancouver (and subsequently other Games) put their questions in the context of the Olympics. In other words, athletes are continually bombarded with messages about how important this *one race* really is. Before any predictions about medals, it's already a pressure cooker.

In addition to an athlete's physical and mental ability with regard to their event, the best chance to stand on an Olympic podium also hinges on their ability to forget about the competition and clear their mind when it's time to rest. I certainly wouldn't bet on the average reporter, high profile or not, appreciating this fact.

But it would help.

* * *

On the first day of the Vancouver Olympics in 2010, Jennifer Heil won a silver medal in the moguls competition. I wrote this on the morning of the event:

> If Jennifer Heil wins a gold medal today and becomes the first Canadian to win gold on home soil, celebrate the fact the drought is over by all means, but don't reduce her

> accomplishment to a trivia question. Winning a gold medal once is a rare feat amongst Olympians. To be in a position to do it again four years later is a rare feat amongst Olympic gold medallists.

Well, it wasn't gold, but it was an amazing performance. I can't think of an athlete who ever faced more pressure leading up to an Olympics. Not once did you see an interview or read an article about her that didn't also refer to the first Canadian gold on home soil. I even heard her referred to as the one "expected" to win it. How would you like to be in that position where anything other than number one in the world would be thought of as a failure?

I was nothing but impressed by Jennifer Heil every time I heard her interviewed and every time I watched her ski. When she was asked if she minded the pressure, she said that's the way she preferred it, which I believe is a difficult mental state to achieve but perhaps what gave her a fighting chance. It's an immense amount of pressure, and when you're "expected" to win *the* gold, as far as the Canadian media was concerned, it's an unfair amount of pressure. But Heil took it on with a smile every time it was mentioned.

I became an even bigger fan of hers because of her performance that night. Under the weight of public expectation, when it mattered most, she threw down an absolutely beautiful run. I'm not a moguls judge, but to my eye it was pretty close to perfect. She did what every athlete dreams of doing, which is having a truly great performance when it matters most. Finishing just behind American Hannah Kearney, another talented athlete with multiple world and Olympic medals, who, like Heil, also had a great day, bears no shame. I can't describe how misguided I find the notion that her performance was somehow a failure.

If the real joy of sport lies in having your best performance in the face of a great challenge, then she and Kearney both did it in a way most of us only wish we could.

* * *

As discussed previously, there is a relationship between what we think and feel and our ability to perform at our best. Especially on a world stage, we know there's going to be pressure, and we know that pressure sometimes contributes to a less than optimal performance. To deal with it, we first need to know how it happens, at least in basic terms.

One of the challenges of a new or bigger competitive environment can be its effect on focus. To perform optimally, you need to be totally focused on what you're attempting to do *here and now.* Living in the "now" is a concept written about extensively in recent years. Eckhardt Tolle, who wrote *The Power of Now,* is probably the most renowned author advocating that we embrace the only way in which we are capable of experiencing the world around us—in the present. How this actually translates to a physical performance is described wonderfully by Dan Millman in his novel *Way of the Peaceful Warrior.* At one point the lead character is literally thrown off a bridge into the water by his mentor. After angrily rushing back up onto the bridge to find out why, he was confronted with this question: "What were you thinking about on the way down?"

The answer, of course, was *nothing* other than how he was going to land. He didn't know he was about to be thrown off the bridge and there was a certain amount of danger involved, so it was a *heightened* experience. This is how high performers experience sport—hyper-aware of the immediate environment and perfectly focused on what they're trying to accomplish. Lights, media, and large crowds add to the distraction at a high-level event. Any fleeting thought relating to either the future or past also serves only as a distraction. If there's even a small part of you aware of what you *don't* want to happen, you're not totally focused on what you *do* want to happen. A version of this concept is trying to *win* versus trying *not to lose.* Trying *not to lose* might not be a conscious decision made by a competitor. It is nonetheless a distraction away from what should be the focus, which is your self-determined game plan.

So far this is a pretty straightforward concept relating to focus. Next you have the compounding effect of a negative thought, which might be the fear of failure or perhaps the fear of injury. This often adds to the problem by creating muscular tension in the body. In Dan Millman's follow up, *The Warrior Athlete,* he illustrates the concept beautifully with this example: The task is to run across a four-inch wide beam as fast as you can, once with the beam a single foot off the ground, and then with the beam fifteen feet off the ground (please don't actually try this). The thought of the *real* possibility of injuring yourself if the second trial is performed unsuccessfully creates muscular tension that impedes your ability to perform the task. The skill required is exactly the same regardless of the height of the beam, therefore the performance is impeded only by a *thought.*

It's also worth pointing out that thoughts don't need to be negative to have a detrimental effect. The Olympic environment can be so wonderful and exciting, especially for someone who has dreamed for years of representing their country. It's *so* exciting, in fact, that it becomes almost impossible for it not to drain your energy, unless you have a good game plan as to how to handle it. This ties back to how difficult the Olympic environment is to simulate. You become immersed in an overwhelmingly positive energy and camaraderie with people you may have even watched *win* medals at previous Games. Then after a few days of being too excited to sleep, at least not as long or as deep as you're used too, it's too late.

An example that illustrates the point well is the four-man bobsleigh from the Torino Olympics. In this race of almost six kilometres in length, Pierre Lueders and crew finished nine hundredths of a second out of the bronze medal position. To be sure, races have been won and lost by smaller margins, but if you look at it in terms of what it would have taken to make up the difference, it doesn't get much closer.

A bobsleigh race involves pushing the sled as fast as you can before jumping in or "loading". The push is measured over a 50m split. At the end of the push, a sled with a faster time typically also has a higher velocity and therefore will continue to gain time on the competition. As a general rule, you can expect the gap to roughly double or even triple in some cases, based solely on the push. So, to make up nine hundredths of a second and win the bronze medal, Pierre's crew needed to push, on average, *one hundredth of a second* faster (or less) in each of the four runs.

This begs the question of whether Pierre's team could have won the bronze if the coaches had moved the best push athlete from another team on to his. The short answer is *yes*. Or more to the point for this discussion, could a member of his team have failed to produce their absolute best performance because they were ever so slightly tired or not fully recuperated? The answer here is also a definitive *yes*. As a matter of fact, it happens in every event, at every Olympics. To be clear, I'm absolutely *not* accusing Pierre's crew of being ill-prepared. They may have had the race of their lives. I use the example only because the math illustrates the point. Races are won and lost by the tiniest of margins. Nerves, pressure, and *excitement,* which we all assume to be only a positive thing, can cause athletes to be off of their best performance by the *tiniest of margins.* This is often what athletes and coaches fail to appreciate, and therefore fail to prepare for.

Now that we have a basic understanding of how pressure and the environment can affect performance, how do we deal with it? Before we get to that, I should begin by pointing out that this is a very personal thing. My job as a national team coach over the years became more and more about the mindset of *individuals.* My comments here are based on my experiences, but it's up to the individual to determine what makes the most sense for them, ideally through trial and error. In other words, athletes need to actually test strategies.

Something I found surprising when I first transitioned into coaching was that the nerves are much more intense for those watching! On more than one occasion, I have thought to myself, *I was never this nervous when it was me out there.* I think my wife would agree with the sentiment, being forced to watch from the sidelines for so many years while I competed. We both remember meeting a few hours prior to my race in Torino; she was unable to hold back the tears, and I did my best to comfort *her.* So why is that? Part of it relates to the participant having an *outlet* for the nerves.

To get ready for an event, athletes warm up and prepare physically, which in combination with mental preparation, regulates muscular tension. A very valuable skill which aids in this process is visualization. Leading up to a race, competitors typically get two training runs per day, which amounts to roughly two minutes of actual sliding on the track. How do we make up for this lack of preparation time? By watching others, analyzing video, walking the track, and more than anything else, visualization.

Good visualization is a skill like any other, and needs to be practiced. It doesn't only include imagining what you would *see,* as the word suggests; it also includes what you would feel. The more vivid the visualization, the more valuable it becomes in terms of both executing a game plan as well as reducing unwanted stress and muscular tension. If your mind is not how you want it to be, perhaps due to nerves or doubts about an upcoming competition, one of the best possible remedies is to visualize the performance you *want* to have.

During a training week in Torino, in preparation for the upcoming Games, I performed over one hundred visualizations for every actual run down the track. To make the process more effective, I watched several hours of video and took high resolution photographs of the track every four or five metres, all the way down. By the time the Olympic race came around, I had only about thirty-five actual training runs. Despite this limitation, I had developed a very strong visual and kinaesthetic game plan I had rehearsed *thousands* of times. As a consequence, both physically and mentally, it was as though I was competing on my home track. I was simultaneously relaxed and extremely focused. I had no excess muscular tension or stress other than what I found useful for the start. On the track, I was hyper-aware of exactly where I was, which allowed me to identify and correct mistakes almost as they happened.

I put a great deal of time and effort into preparing for the race, and as a consequence I was able to execute my game plan. In hindsight, I can think of only one moment during the competition in which I might have wanted to be in a slightly different position on the track. It wasn't perfect, but it was about as close as you get in the sport of skeleton, at least in my judgement.

At the time I thought of myself as someone who was simply good at handling pressure. Certainly my perspective about competition and the fact I had been competing in a variety of sports for so many years played a role, but if you asked me about my ability in this regard now, I would describe it differently. *Now* I would say I had done a very good job of minimizing the effects of pressure through extensive visualization and various other strategies. I also have an appreciation for the fact that preparation and/or handling pressure is specific to the environment, as opposed to a general trait an individual does or does not possess.

Here's a quick story to illustrate the point. Years after the Torino Olympics, my teammate and friend Kelly and I were at what was then called the Lindsay Park Sports Centre in Calgary (now the Repsol Sports Centre). It was over the Christmas holidays and both of our families were out of town. It was also Kelly's birthday so at one point when we were in the pool area Kelly informed me he had decided what he wanted from me in lieu of a gift. I was to go to the top of the ten metre diving tower, sit on the edge, push down with my hands so that my body was suspended in the air with only my hands in contact with the platform, and then push off and land in the water. My first inclination was that this would be easy until Kelly added slyly that most people who tried this ended up rotating forward and belly flopping into the pool.

To make a long story short, I eventually performed the task without incident. But the experience was an eye-opener. The thought of landing on my stomach was vivid, and despite the fact that I practiced the skill on every platform, working my way eventually to the top, I was literally shaking with nerves by the time I went. I still remember being struck by how close I was to the roof of the facility when I was on the top level of the diving tower. Only one person at a time is allowed up there and Kelly and I still laugh about how long I took and how there were young kids calling up at me shouting, "Come on! Go already!"

So why was that such a difficult experience to manage? A belly flop from 10 metres would be extremely painful but certainly the risk was less than what I experienced as a skeleton athlete on a regular basis. Perhaps not in the same manner, but I had jumped off that same tower on a number of other occasions without really giving it a second thought. As I said, I thought of myself as someone who handled pressure really well, but in essence, this was an experience in which I had no time to access any of the coping strategies that had worked so well for me as an athlete. And without an outlet for my fear and nerves, the tension built up and made the whole experience quite unpleasant. On the other hand, it wasn't unpleasant for Kelly. He still brings it up now and then as one of his favourite birthday memories.

So preparation is number one. Do your homework, do your training, and make visualization a big part of your preparation. In the sliding sports, we rely very heavily on visualization but don't be fooled into thinking that it's only about remembering when and where to steer. That's certainly a part of it, but the effect on the body has clear implications for any sport. It's a great way of stopping negative thoughts and putting yourself in an optimal state mentally, which of course then has an effect on your physical state as well.

* * *

I want to conclude this chapter by mentioning two additional strategies that worked very effectively for me over my competitive career. The first relates to the quote at the beginning of this chapter from Catriona Le May Doan. There absolutely will be pressure. In my experience, athletes spend a great deal of time trying to almost *trick* themselves in to believing they aren't nervous, whether that's with breathing techniques, centring, meditation, or visualization. But can you really trick yourself? Aren't you just pretending you're not nervous? I believe at some level you need to acknowledge it's there and just deal with it.

Leading up to Torino, I knew it was my last chance at an Olympic medal. Through various muscle pulls and the fact I was absolutely exhausted at the end of the previous two competitive seasons, my body was telling me my career was nearing its end. Having won the test event on the same track the year before, I knew I had a good chance to be on the podium, but this just added to the pressure I felt. For months leading into my last Olympics as an athlete, I anticipated the pressure in Torino would be greater than anything I had experienced to that point in my career. And I knew I needed to face it and acknowledge it.

The one previous experience I had in Salt Lake City was different in that no one would have considered me a medal threat. *I* believed I had a chance, but back then I had won only one World Cup medal and had not performed well in any previous (or subsequent) competitions on the Salt Lake City track. I knew it would be different this time, and so my strategy needed to be different as well.

I had to perform under the weight of my expectations, so rather than using various techniques to minimize the pressure, I *invited it in.* I reasoned that any nerves I felt on the road to the Olympics would pale in comparison to the nerves I would face when I got there. So any time I felt even a hint of the butterflies, I didn't try to get rid of them. I actually tried to make myself feel them *more.* I focused on them, what they felt like in my stomach, in my muscles, and in my lungs. And then the strangest thing happened—they began to fade away.

It reminds me of how the same thing happens whenever I try to force an emotion. Have you ever tried to laugh at someone's joke when it *wasn't* funny, just to be polite? It's a struggle! Or tried not to laugh at a time or place where it wasn't appropriate, like when you were in school and on the verge of being sent to the principal's office? That's when it becomes almost impossible *not* to laugh. I *tried* to feel as nervous as I possibly could and I couldn't do it! Now I'm not saying I didn't *feel* nervous, but I wanted to feel it to a much greater extent because I wanted to prove to myself I could still execute my best game plan whether I was nervous or not. As it turned out, I inadvertently found an effective strategy at eliminating the vast majority of the nerves I had. I can't be certain if it will work for others as it did for me, but I believe strongly that any strategy must involve acknowledging the nerves and accepting them, and then going from there.

The second strategy relates to an experience I had competing one summer with the Toronto Argonauts Rowing Club. I took up rowing during my undergrad at Western and dreamed of representing my country at the Olympics like my uncle Ted had done at the 1984 Games in Los Angeles. On this particular occasion, I was nervous about an upcoming race with our four-man crew, nervous to the point that it crossed my mind that I'd rather not be there. We were tired from previous races and the weather was cold and rainy. The race would be a real challenge and perhaps it was beyond our ability to win. And then for some reason, it didn't happen.

I honestly don't remember if the event was cancelled or postponed but suddenly we went from competing to not getting the *chance* to compete. That was a very valuable experience for me because my reaction was immediate frustration and anger. Almost instantly I went from nerves and fear that were so strong I wished I was somewhere else to being right pissed off that we couldn't race. Every time I felt nerves from that point forward, I remembered that day and I asked myself which was worse: the stress and the nerves and anxiety of sport or not being given such a beautiful opportunity to face a challenge.

I realize using this particular strategy would be much easier if you've actually had an experience like I did, swinging so quickly from one extreme to another. But I believe it's still valuable to ask yourself in that moment of stress, "How would you feel right now if you were prevented from competing?" As I sit writing this now, with my competitive days behind me, it seems all the more poignant.

Think of it like this: Do kids grow up dreaming about being on the bench when Michael Jordan takes the game-winning shot? No. They dream about *taking* the shot. They dream they *are* Michael Jordan. It takes guts to take the shot, and sometimes the nerves make you wonder if you wouldn't rather be somewhere else. But "there would be no triumph in success if there had been no hazard in failure."

Face those great challenges in sport while you can. Because that is truly *living the dream.*

Duff Gibson

15. About the Journey

"Medals, they go and they sit on your mantle or they go and they sit in your sock drawer."

—Randy Gregg, 5-time Stanley Cup winner

If you aspire to be a champion, you very likely spend time imagining what it'll be like. Dreaming about it and just believing it's possible are necessary steps in the process, but it's easy to be so focused on the future you fail to fully experience and appreciate the present.

When we use clichés like *it's about the journey* or *enjoy the process,* it doesn't mean we shouldn't visualize success. Clearly there's a great benefit to doing so. It *does* mean that to be successful at anything, you have to spend a great many hours, the overwhelming majority of your time in fact, developing and perfecting your abilities. In other words, we spend so much *more* time preparing for competition than we do competing. It's not possible to work so hard for so long to reach the highest level if you don't love what you do. It's important, every once in a while, to remember and acknowledge this fact.

Many retired athletes refer to their competitive days as the best of their lives. If I could give advice to the younger version of myself, it would be to enjoy such a beautiful and uncomplicated time in your life *while it's happening*. An athlete or anyone who wants to achieve something great needs to be goal-oriented and needs to dream about and/or visualize success, but focusing on the future too often can cause you to miss some of the joy in *chasing* the dream.

On two separate occasions, before I was born, my father won the Canadian Open Judo Championships. After the second time, he and my mother were walking out of the venue with trophy in hand. As trophies sometimes are, this one was very tall and elaborate with many levels, one of which had a platform supporting a series of gold balls upon which another platform sat, and so on. I mention this because, as they were walking out, my mom, who was carrying the trophy, slipped and fell, smashing it into a million pieces. My father described a vivid memory of all the little gold balls rolling into a sewer.

According to my father, my mother cried when this happened. As a young person, this made sense to me. She had just destroyed the prize, the main reason for doing a sport in the first place. My dad, on the other hand, described it as if it was this beautiful and hilarious memory. This part did *not* make sense.

I was baffled that he could actually find humour in it, and when I asked him why he was laughing, his response was, "Why would I worry about something that was going to end up in a cardboard box in the basement anyway?" As you might imagine, I was absolutely disappointed with his explanation and couldn't understand how he could feel the way he did. Now, after so many years of competing in sport and having had my share of success and failure, I understand much better what he meant. Besides his default position that sport was ultimately of little consequence, his point in this case was that a trophy is just a symbol. If you take away the symbol, it doesn't change what happened or what you went through to make it happen. It doesn't change the *journey*.

A trophy or any kind of award is always secondary to the real benefit of sport or why we might choose to chase a dream in the first place. I used to think if I won an Olympic medal, I would be very protective of it. I imagined I would keep it in a safety deposit box or perhaps in a safe if I had it around the house at all. But I confused the symbol with the act itself and everything that went into making it happen.

In preparation for this chapter, I asked a number of athletes, some *with* and some *without* an Olympic medal, if they would do it all again if they knew they would *not* win. I was surprised at how consistently the answer, without hesitation, was "yes". As a parent now I sometimes think of the same question from a different perspective: would you want your kids to participate knowing they would never make a national team or play a professional sport? My wife and I certainly would. Why? Because we have an appreciation for the process and the great value in all the lessons learned along the way.

Whether you look at this as an athlete or coach or perhaps as a parent, if we all had a greater appreciation for the value of the journey, we might act differently. We each have the ability to make life enjoyable or miserable for ourselves and for the people around us. If we saw the value in the journey instead of this overwhelming focus on the end-goal, we might be more appreciative of it for its own sake. We might have more respect for our opponents and we would very likely be more successful as well, because we'd work together to reach a higher level than any one of us would be capable of in isolation. The best coaches my kids ever had were all about personal development. One went so far as to say that baseball was only the venue through which he taught other things, like work ethic, sportsmanship, and teamwork—all of which in turn make you a better baseball player! It's not a complicated idea.

I was very lucky in my athletic career to have a great support system, of which my wife played the leading role. I also had great teammates and great competitors who all played a part in both my enjoyment of sport and ultimately the level of success I achieved. What is often overlooked and was foundational to my success was the fact that my teammates, coaches, and competitors were people of character. They didn't make it miserable; they made it even more enjoyable for me to be there and they collectively created an environment in which I thrived and was able to achieve my best.

To this day, I am grateful.

* * *

There's a section in Andre Agassi's book *Open* in which he talks about winning his first Major. Prior to that he had been in a number of finals without winning and had really taken a beating in the press for being too much about *image* and not having what it takes to be the best. When it finally happened for him, it seemed like the press did an abrupt about-face and instantly he could do no wrong. Knowing he was the same person as he was prior to winning a Major, and having everything seem so different in terms of how people related to him, the whole experience really opened his eyes.

> I'm supposed to be a different person now that I've won a slam. Everyone says so. After two years of calling me a fraud, a choke artist, a rebel without a cause, they lionize me. They declare that I'm a winner, a player of substance, the real deal. They say my victory at Wimbledon forces them to reassess me to reconsider who I really am. But I don't feel that

> Wimbledon has changed me. I feel, in fact, as if I've been let in on a dirty little secret: winning changes nothing.

Imagine what that would be like. You wake up one day and everyone treats you differently, *better*, and you're exactly the same person. Agassi even admits it wasn't his greatest performance and his victory was at least partially due to his opponent making mistakes at the wrong moments. Knowing it could have gone either way, and knowing it could have gone either way in previous matches when he lost, and having everyone act like he was now a different person, gave him a really interesting perspective.

He goes on to say that he felt *bad* after losing, a lot longer than he felt *good* after winning. It's almost as if winning isn't all it's cracked up to be. Because winning the big one is something all athletes dream about, sometimes for decades, it's very difficult for the experience to live up to the hype. That's why I believe at the highest level, very successful athletes are all about the challenge, and in certain circumstances they're even more about the challenge than the actual victory. In other words, the greatest fulfillment sometimes comes from the journey rather than the destination. Sometimes the destination is fulfilling only through the lens of what it took to get there.

So strive for the top, absolutely. Dream about it. Do what it takes. Work hard on improving mentally and physically, but also realize that by just *trying* to improve and *trying* to be the best, you're experiencing something you'll look back on with great reverie. Not everyone has the privilege of dedicating themselves to a singular pursuit. Don't let the fact that only a few ever reach the top interfere with what a wonderful journey it can be.

* * *

Torino in 2006 was the culmination of my athletic career. It would be inaccurate for me to say I never dreamed I could win a medal at the Olympics because I had dreamed about it since I was a kid. Like any kid, I didn't know if it was possible. But unlike most kids, I didn't know *or care* what sport it would be in and I was willing to try almost anything to chase the dream.

After years of training and competing in a variety of sports, I tried skeleton and it was a perfect fit. It was the one sport whose demands aligned exactly with my own strengths and weaknesses and I became internationally competitive after only a few years. I was able to transfer a significant amount of my previous training, that from bobsleigh being the most applicable, such that after a relatively short career of six years on the national team, and having benefited greatly from good timing and almost ideal circumstances, relating most significantly to the people I went through the experience with, my Olympic dream came true.

In December of 2009 as the coach of the national "B" team, I returned for the first time to the venue where it all happened. I was a little nervous to see it again, wondering if I would feel some kind of heightened emotion left over from that day. But, if anything, the opposite was true. Being there in some ways refreshed aspects of the memory, but what struck me more than anything was how different it looked and how much things had changed in *my* life.

At the venue, what was most obviously missing were the temporary stands around the start and finish areas. The Olympics are different from any other sporting event because of the incredible atmosphere resulting from and being reflected back by the people in attendance and the people you know are on the other side of the cameras. On this day, there weren't the same competitors, officials, spectators, media, or support staff, let alone family and friends. What remained was the track itself and the land upon which it was built, but not much else. The Torino Olympics seemed a more distant memory to me then despite the fact that less than four years had passed.

Before every race in skeleton, we have a team captains' meeting to discuss safety issues, logistics, and to organize the order of training. During the meeting on this occasion, I found myself staring at a banner at the front of the room with the slogan from the Games—*Passion Lives Here.* The banner reminded me how important the Olympics were to me then. That one day—February 17, 2006—was a huge part of my life and my sole focus as an athlete for the four years since the closing ceremonies of the Salt Lake City Olympics in 2002. There were tokens and mementos from the Olympics all around the track, and it occurred to me that if you walked into my house back in Calgary, you would see less evidence of the race.

So what's my point? That I've somehow outgrown it? No. It was a wonderful time in my life and I still feel grateful that circumstances unfolded as they did and I had the opportunity to give it my all. In writing this I am reminded of an article written by Randy Starkman, someone I admire greatly and who is missed tremendously in the world of amateur sport since his passing. Randy saw sport from a much higher level, and the article was summarized quite nicely by a quote from five-time Stanley Cup winner Randy Gregg who said, "Medals, they go and they sit on your mantle or they go and they sit in your sock drawer."

Medals do end up in your sock drawer! Again, I'm not implying in any way that it wasn't a great time in my life or that it wasn't really important to me, because it was and remains so. But looking back now, I see it was as much about the journey as it was the destination. When I think about skeleton, that last Olympic race is not usually what comes to mind first. I prefer to remember the camaraderie and the laughs we had. While I was still competing I undervalued the journey because the focus was always the destination. If you have the presence of mind to realize the greatest benefit and enjoyment is found in the process, *while it's actually happening*, as opposed to being tied into whether or not you actually achieve your goal, then you've really got something.

Being back at the venue for the first time since the Olympics brought back some great memories. But like every one of us at different moments in our lives, I'm enjoying a different journey now.

* * *

My all-time favourite quote about the mindset of a champion comes from Olympic rower Marnie McBean who said, "My impression of Olympic gold medallists plummeted when I won one myself." Before she won her first Olympic gold, Marnie assumed, like anyone might, that winning one was a superhuman feat that took some kind of special talent or knowledge that nobody else had. Essentially, her experience proved the assumption wrong. Certainly a number of factors have to align, and for me luck played a significant role several times along the way, but winning an Olympic medal is clearly not impossible and it's not superhuman. To quote Marnie again, it's "ordinary people doing extraordinary things". The whole experience has left me with the realization that the people most worthy of our admiration may or may not be champions at what they do.

Max Thompson was a Nordic-combined skier at the Torino Olympics, and like myself was staying in the Olympic Village in Sestrière. I had seen Max a few times in the lounge watching other athletes compete, but the first time we ever had a conversation was in the dining hall a few days after my race. I was sitting with my teammate Paul and the Australian skeleton coach, a retired American slider by the name of Terry Holland, as well as a few hundred other athletes and coaches from around the world. Keep in mind the media had played up the fact that I was a firefighter and had just set a record for being the oldest person to win a gold medal in an individual sport at the Winter Olympics. Max walked over to us, put his hand up to give me a high five and said, "Hey man, I just saw your bio: firefighter, gold medal, senior citizen. All right!"

There was definitely a part of me that thought, *am I giving a high five to someone who just called me a senior citizen?* But I couldn't help but immediately like him, and I'm sure Paul and Terry felt the same way based on the delight they took at Max's comment. In fact, later that year Paul had a t-shirt made for my birthday with the words "Firefighter. Gold Medal. Senior Citizen." imprinted on it. Think about what kind of person Max would have to be to do that. How many twenty-one-year-olds could walk over to a complete stranger almost twice their age, who had just won the Olympics, and give that line?

Several days later, on the night of the closing ceremonies, I ran into Max again. He was actually leaving the party at the main village, which didn't make sense to me. If there was anyone who should be enjoying the party it's a young single guy who's just finished his first Olympics. He mentioned he was looking for someone: a Nordic-combined official from another country. I asked him why and he said that he had been relying on this person for the past season to transport his ski jumping skis from competition to competition because he couldn't afford the extra baggage charges. He wanted to show his gratitude by giving her his Olympic team jacket.

That was an eye-opener for me. As amateur athletes, we often complain about financial support, looking at the few countries in the world that fund sport to a larger extent. Personally I think we should fund sport more, especially at the grassroots level. To my way of thinking, sport is preventative health care. If we invest more money in sport, more of our athletes excel, more and more kids are inspired to participate, and ultimately more people lead active lives. As a nation, we become healthier. But I'm admittedly biased.

In any case, I've certainly complained about a lack of funding from time to time, but in reality, at least in Torino, I was in a pretty good position. There wasn't anything I wish I had but couldn't afford that would have made my preparation better for the Games. And in contrast there was Max, a member of the same Olympic team, who was a *skier* who couldn't afford to travel *with skis.* If my skeleton career had been the same way, I don't know what I would have done. I can't say for certain I would have stuck with it long enough to reach the level I did.

We all have our own journey and some of us face more significant challenges than others. Some of us are successful in part because of circumstances or because we're simply better suited to what we do. Having met Max, and having had the experience I did in Salt Lake City where I didn't have the race I had dreamed of, I have come to appreciate character on an equal footing and sometimes to a greater extent than talent or success. Because of his journey, I admire Max and what he's had to endure and the character he showed to make it to that level.

Would I admire him more if he had won an Olympic medal? Nope.

16. Pass It On

"To make a difference is not a matter of accident, a matter of casual occurrence of the tides. People choose to make a difference."

—Maya Angelou

Many years ago when I was in grade five, we had a sports day in which the last event was a mass start cross-country race involving the whole school. With four or five hundred metres to go, the leader of the race was a sixth-grade kid named Bell. He was the Scarborough champion at the time, and as expected, he ended up winning easily. What wasn't expected, at least by me, was that after perhaps three quarters of the race, I was in fourth place, just a few metres behind third and maybe about thirty or forty metres behind second.

From that point, the course went around a soccer field and two baseball diamonds before heading to the finish line. My father had come to watch and was sitting on a hill overlooking the playing fields. I had seen him there, and like any kid I wanted to perform at my best, knowing he was watching. The odd thing was I *thought* I was doing great. I was a fifth grade kid beating all but a few of the sixth-graders. Then my father yelled my name and after a slight pause added, "Go!" It startled me and I don't remember exactly how or why I was so motivated, but I did what he said. I thought I was working hard to that point, but when my father yelled out to me, I was able to push myself harder than I ever had before. I passed the kid who was immediately in front of me and slowly started making inroads towards second place.

I was chasing one of those kids who, in my mind at least, was practically a grown man in grade six! We all thought of him as the toughest kid in the school and, aside from Bell, the best athlete as well. Gradually over the entire distance, I caught up and in the end tied for second place after a long, all-out sprint to the finish. To my pre-adolescent mind, the greatest moment of the whole experience was when a classmate ran over to me to say he had overheard the kid I tied say that I was "fast as hell". We considered "hell" a swear word at the time. It seems funny thinking back on it now, but to that point in my life it was the highlight of my athletic career.

The true value of the experience was that it was the first time I pushed through my perceived limits. I learned something that day about myself. I thought I was giving a good effort, and I *was* in relation to my expectations, but clearly not in relation to my ability. Would I have learned that lesson if my father hadn't been at the race that day? Perhaps eventually, but likely not as well or as early on in my sporting career.

* * *

A friend of mine named Bob is now in his mid-eighties. Believe it or not, until quite recently he still played tennis every week with a few equally ageless friends. A while ago now we were talking about sportsmanship and the value of sport, and it caused him to think back to a time in his youth when he attended Ridley College in St. Catharines, Ontario. In an email he recounted an experience that has stuck with him throughout his life.

> At the same school with the sports motto as mentioned previously [it's not whether you win or lose, but how you play the game], there was a football match being played against our arch-rival. Well, you have heard of the old sleeper play where you take three players off the field and send back two into the huddle hoping the opposition doesn't notice the missing player crouched down near the sideline pretending to be part of the crowd. Well this is what our team did and it looked like the trick was going to work when out of the crowd near the crouching lad came this bustling old man dressed in his suit and black teaching gown and wielding his cane high above his head. He gave the lad a couple of good licks with the cane while yelling in his booming voice, "We don't play like this at Ridley! We don't play like this at Ridley!" It was the dreaded headmaster. Well, whether we won the game or not I cannot recall but the lesson of "play the game fairly and properly", as I said before, was reinforced and has lasted me a lifetime.

It's not enough to simply enrol our youth and hope they learn the great lessons sport has to teach. As parents, coaches, and even as senior members within a team, we need to take an active role to ensure the right lessons are reinforced and the negative behaviours discouraged. It's too easy to forget why it exists in the first place or why we would want our children to participate.

There are undoubtedly those who would argue that the "old sleeper play" isn't breaking any rules, and getting caught by it is a valuable lesson in its own right. Times have certainly changed since Bob attended Ridley College. Hitting a kid with a cane wasn't unusual back then, and certainly the majority of people would oppose the practice now, but you can't argue the headmaster didn't have a clear understanding of *his* role. My fear is there are fewer people out there who would take the same action today. In fairness, I don't know how I would react. I'd like to think I know, but what the headmaster did took courage. Take a moment and think about it. He stopped a high school football game to make a point about fair play and actually *earning* what you achieve.

It's *exactly* the kind of thing a young football player would never forget. And it's perfectly aligned with the greater purpose of sport, and school sport in particular, which is to build character and teach values. This is an absolutely beautiful illustration of the positive impact an individual can have on a young person. It's a lesson that has served Bob, and I'd imagine the vast majority of his teammates, close to seventy years now.

At the end of his story, Bob added what might be the highest compliment a headmaster could receive. He said, "And I have tried to live my life by this standard."

For those who strive to be a positive force in the world, one can only dream.

* * *

Earlier in this book, I included a short essay written by Neil Crone, a comedian, actor, writer, and a former high school football player coached by my father. The following was actually the first piece written by Neil and it speaks to the purpose of sport in teaching values and how we have the ability to affect the lives of those around us. I extend an absolutely heartfelt thank you to Neil from myself and the rest of my family for this beautiful gift.

> I went to my high school reunion last month. I was excited about going. It's been twenty-five years since I graduated and

there are many old friends that I dearly wanted to see again. Unfortunately, although well organized and held at a lovely venue, the reunion for some inexplicable reason was poorly attended. From my entire graduating class I met a little over a dozen people. Still, it was nice to see their smiling and aging faces. There were many wonderful surprises and not a few ghastly shocks. It's amazing how far south the human body can go in a couple of decades. The highlight of my evening though, with the exception of having a glass of red wine spilled down my back by some class of '69 piss-tank and being relentlessly hounded by a stoned beatnik desperate to engage me in a dialogue of souls, was a chance to sit with my old friend and football coach, Andy.

Andy has always has been a great bull of a man. As high school football players flopping about spastically in ill-fitting uniforms, we were often terrified by his baleful glare and his booming voice. He didn't say much but if he was addressing you, chances were you'd screwed up. If we were lazy or in need of correction he would make us do chin ups in full gear from the goal posts. He lived for rainy days when he could make us practice running and diving in the mud, until we were soggy through to the skin. At practice's end we would stagger back to the locker room looking like the days survivors from some catastrophic flood.

Still, we loved him. There are dozens of us here today who once shared a huddle who would still run through a brick wall for him. The reasons for our devotion are admittedly clichéd but nonetheless timeless. Through Andy and with Andy we learned about courage, pride, loyalty and how to be good men. I'm not sure they still teach those things. I hope to

God they do. I hope to God my own boys are sent an Andy that they will gladly sweat and ache for.

On this night though, Andy and I did not talk much football. We came together as veterans of the cancer gridiron, both of us engaged in the games of our lives, mine only just begun, his already into a well-fought and exhausting overtime. Typically Andy was not conceding any easy yardage. He was making his cancer hang from the crossbar and dive through the mud.

I have a particularly vivid memory from my days in high school. I'm lying face down on a hospital gurney, stabbed in the leg while attempting to stop a thief from robbing the gym locker rooms and in great pain and scared to death. In the midst of my panic I am aware that a strong hand is holding mine, calming me down, helping me to be brave. It was Andy. I never knew when or how he got there but there he was.

As we said good-bye that night at the reunion, perhaps for the last time, I made sure to take his hand and squeeze it for just a little longer than necessary hoping to give him back some of the courage he so freely and so often gave to me.

—Neil Crone

* * *

At the grassroots level, sport is volunteer-driven. As such it remains inconsistent in terms of the experience it provides a young person. There will always be some absolutely wonderful coaches who teach values and inspire a love of the game, as well as those who are less inclined to do so. Either way, coaching is typically a short term commitment for parents as their own kids age out and/or move on to other things. There are always lessons learned, for athletes and coaches alike, but do they get passed along?

When my kids were younger, I wanted for them the coach who could teach them the most about their sport. After many years of them each playing two or three sports per year, we really only had one or two negative experiences, but they were powerful reminders that a desire to play is more important than what a coach can teach about skating or batting. Sport is only the *venue.* Sport is the *mode* through which lessons of greater value are taught. Age group, as well as school sport, *exist* for a purpose quite apart from creating great athletes.

I feel as though there's a segment of youth sport going down a specific path, in part because of a *misperception,* when there's no need for it. Here's what we know for sure: in youth sport if it's too much about the win, you run the risk of taking the fun out of it. We *know* the majority of those who quit do so because it's too serious and it's not fun anymore. If we make it about growth, whether in terms of skill development or the values we hope to instil, that doesn't conflict with an athlete's enjoyment at all. In fact, when you make progress, you gain a little confidence, a little pride maybe, you get a sense of satisfaction and these things are motivating, and this is also *exactly* in line with the mindset of an elite athlete! In other words, you focus on process more and outcome less, and you win more often as well. So why wouldn't you?

Even the most demanding coach would have to acknowledge the value in instilling a love of the game. So many of the all-time greats from every professional sport would tell you it all started with friends playing on the street, in a park, or in a sandlot. Is that by accident? Absolutely not. Is it enough? No, but if you look at how it translates to an active and healthy lifestyle, in and of itself, it's a wonderful thing. And it's also perfectly in line with the mindset that makes achieving a higher level of success that much more likely.

Sport has the capacity to be a very powerful force in the world, but to an individual at any given moment in time, it can be either good or bad. It's not *inherently* positive. It's up to those who lead to *make* it so. That's why it's critically important to take the time to consider the purpose of sport and the experience an individual or an organization wants to inspire. It's a tremendous responsibility to have such sway in the lives of young people when the repercussions, good or bad, can be felt for decades. That's one of my hopes for this book—to get parents, coaches, athletes, and organizations to consider their purpose, and to then be *purposeful* in making it happen.

In an earlier chapter, I included a quote from Ralph Waldo Emerson. The *beautiful compensation* to which he refers is the fact that you also help yourself when you sincerely try to help another. Something that might also qualify is how a coach invests in character development, and with no additional effort gets a better athlete. This is only possible because how we *think* affects how we learn, how we challenge ourselves, and how we *grow.* Without question, there is a *Tao,* a way of being, that lends itself to personal success in sport and certainly beyond sport as well.

This book is what I've found to be true through my experiences as a graduate student working with high performance athletes, as an athlete, as a coach, and as a parent. I've had a front row seat to some incredible performances, both on and off the podium, and both on and off the field of play. Each athlete and each performance teaches, and there's great value there that I hope I've been able to communicate effectively.

Of course, there will always be some negative in sport, be it a scandal or someone cheating. But the beauty of sport remains, because in the final analysis it's more about you challenging *you*. That's why cheating defeats the purpose. It's about being the best version of yourself, and that's true of athletes at any level.

For a select few being your best means a medal or a championship. As a society this is what we focus almost all of our attention on. But for even the top competitors there was first a longer period of time when they weren't a medal threat at all. In truth, they were no different than so many of us, just working to get better and chasing our passion.

And for those of us whose competitive days are over, without the prize dangling out front, often *skewing* our perception of why we participate, it's so easy to see the true value of sport in the world. If you're one of the lucky ones who never had the fun taken out of it, then you are very likely still motivated by a challenge, and still playing for the love of the game.

Please pass it on.

Acknowledgments

This book was well over a decade in the making and represents a lifetime of learning and experiencing what sport has to teach us in its many forms. As is reflected in the dedication, the credit goes to mom and dad initially for helping me to find my passion, and then to all the people in leadership positions, the great teammates, and great competitors who contributed so much to an environment that facilitated my passion and my continued desire to learn and grow.

As I have described in the book, living in Calgary amongst such tremendous thinkers and doers, who are both brilliant and humble, has been such a gift over the years. I am indebted to each of you. Thank you specifically to those whom I reached out to for their time and input with this book. For your beautiful and wonderful written contributions, thank you to Neil Crone, Clara Hughes, Neal Marshall, and Ben Rutledge. For your time, thoughts, and feedback, thank you to Dr. Cari Din, Max Gartner, Kristina Groves, Dr. Steve Norris, Dr. Cal Botterill, Ron McLean, Beckie Scott, Kyle Shewfelt, Jason Dorland, Dr. Matt Jordan, and Dr. David Legg.

I am also grateful to those individuals I reached out to for support. In a few cases we had never met before, but from what I knew of you, I thought you might really support the message. I think it's an important one and I'm grateful that you did too. Thank you to Dan Jansen, Catriona Le May Doan, Erica Wiebe, Lascelles Brown, Carol Huynh, Rilee ManyBears, and Steve Mesler.

On the technical end, because this was my first experience writing a book, thank you to all those who helped me navigate the unknown territory. Thank you for sharing your personal experiences with writing and publishing to help me figure out what might be the best path for me. Only time will tell, but I'm very comfortable with the decisions I've made based on your input, so thank you.

In terms of editing, in and of itself, it's been such a valuable experience. I've learned a great deal from Elliott Cockram who did the lion's share of the work, "zooming in and zooming out" to provide some great insight. Elliott has also been invaluable setting up the formatting and providing direction with the various steps one needs to negotiate to produce a good finished product. He also let me know that phrases like "steps one needs to negotiate" is archaic and should be avoided, which I almost always did.

A special thanks to Todd Howard who volunteered to read and offer his feedback about the book prior to interviewing me on his Salish Wolf podcast. Something I've found to be a challenge is finding the balance between taking advice from very experienced and knowledgeable people who have varying perspectives relating to the book, and what I need to do to remain true to my vision. It helped a lot that Todd's feedback was right in line with what Elliott had suggested which, of course, is just better peace of mind for me.

Thanks again to everyone mentioned here or in the book itself for being so valuable to me first as an athlete and coach, and then in the process of writing. Despite the fact I've been consistently *optimistic* in my predictions as to when a final product would become available, I know it's been worth the effort and the book is much better than it would have otherwise been without each of you.

About the Author

In 1989, having completed his undergrad at Western, Duff Gibson moved to Calgary to earn his master's degree in kinesiology at the University of Calgary and begin a twenty-five year journey in high performance sport. As an athlete, Duff was a World Champion in 2004 and an Olympic Champion at the Torino Games in 2006 in the sport of skeleton. Duff was also named Canada's male athlete of the year for 2006. In his four years as the national team head coach, Duff led six different athletes to the podium at a World Cup or World Championship level and considers the work they did on mindset and collaboration as being the key to their success. Having moved on from coaching after the 2014 Sochi Olympics, Duff launched Dark Horse Athletic in early 2016. Dark Horse is about developing physical literacy, a growth mindset, and, above all, inspiring kids to participate for the love of sport. Duff lives with his wife Jen and sons Geddy and Taye in Calgary and is a captain with the Calgary Fire Department.

Made in the USA
Monee, IL
04 October 2021

78962946R00125